Liz Mohn Stiftung, Bertelsmann Stiftung (Hrsg./eds.)

Das globale Dorf mit 100 Menschen
The global village of 100 people

| BertelsmannStiftung

| Verlag BertelsmannStiftung

Bibliografische Information der Deutschen Nationalbibliothek

Bibliographic information published by the Deutsche Nationalbibliothek

Die Deutsche Nationalbibliothek verzeichnet diese Publikation in der
Deutschen Nationalbibliografie; detaillierte bibliografische Daten
sind im Internet unter http://dnb.dnb.de abrufbar.
The Deutsche Nationalbibliothek lists this publication in the
Deutsche Nationalbibliografie; detailed bibliographic data
is available on the Internet at http://dnb.dnb.de.

© 2025 Verlag Bertelsmann Stiftung, Gütersloh
Autoren/Authors: Simon Paul Balzert, Sanny Adam Pulka
Verantwortlich/Responsible: Matthias Meis
Lektorat/Copy editors: Heike Herrberg, Bielefeld / Tim Schroder, Frankfurt a. M.
Übersetzung/Translation: Tim Schroder, Frankfurt a. M.
Herstellung/Production editor: Christiane Raffel
Artdirektion/Art-direction: David Bärwald
Gestaltung, Illustration/Design, Illustration: Paul Feldkamp
Bildnachweis/Photo credits: Jan Voth (S. 5), PicturePeople (S. 7)
Druck/Printing: Hans Gieselmann Druck und Medienhaus GmbH & Co. KG, Bielefeld

ISBN 978-3-68933-004-0 (Print/print)
ISBN 978-3-68933-005-7 (E-Book PDF/e-book PDF)

Verlag Bertelsmann Stiftung
Carl-Bertelsmann-Str. 256
D-33311 Gütersloh
verlag@bertelsmann-stiftung.de
www.bertelsmann-stiftung.de/verlag
www.bertelsmann-stiftung.org/publications

Inhalt
Contents

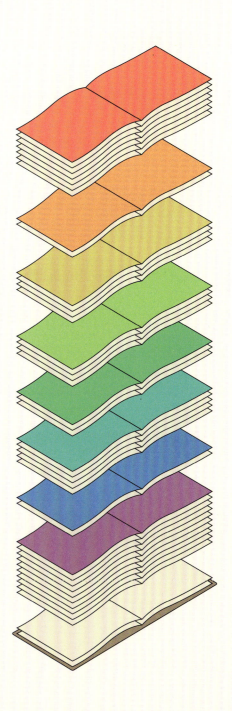

1. Kontinente / Continents
2. Länder / Countries
3. Alter / Age
4. Muttersprachen / Native languages
5. Weltsprachen / World languages
6. Religion / Religion
7. Wohnort / Place of residence
8. Armenviertel / Slums
9. Analphabetismus / Illiteracy
10. Bildung / Education
11. Arbeit / Work
12. Einkommen / Income
13. Vermögen / Assets
14. Bankkonto / Bank account
15. Krankenversicherung / Health insurance
16. Psychische Gesundheit / Mental health
17. Fleischkonsum / Meat consumption
18. Laktoseintoleranz / Lactose intolerance
19. Übergewicht / Overweight
20. Unterernährung / Malnutrition
21. Toiletten / Toilets
22. Sauberes Trinkwasser / Clean drinking water
23. Elektrizität / Electricity
24. Waschmaschinen / Washing machines
25. Internet / Internet
26. Reisen ins Ausland / Travel abroad
27. Smartphones / Smartphones
28. Autos / Cars
29. CO_2-Emissionen / CO_2 emissions
30. Bedrohung durch den Klimawandel / Threats from climate change
31. Leben in Konfliktregionen / Life in conflict regions
32. Demokratien und Autokratien / Democracies and autocracies
33. Sicherheit / Safety
34. Bürgerliche Freiheiten / Civil liberties
35. Zugang zum Rechtsstaat / Access to rule of law
36. Akademische Freiheit / Academic freedom
37. Pressefreiheit / Freedom of the press
38. Korruption / Corruption
39. Geschlechtergerechtigkeit / Gender equality
40. Gleichgeschlechtliche Ehe / Same-sex marriage

Vorwort
Preface

Liebe Leserin, lieber Leser,

mehr als acht Milliarden Menschen leben auf unserem Planeten. Ausgeschrieben ist das eine Acht mit neun Nullen: 8.000.000.000. Jede:r von uns ist eine dieser Personen und trotzdem fällt es uns schwer, Statistiken zur Weltbevölkerung auf uns zu beziehen. Anders sieht es aus, wenn wir die gesamte Weltbevölkerung auf ein globales Dorf herunterrechnen: Wenn die Welt nicht acht Milliarden, sondern nur 100 Bewohner:innen hätte, wird anschaulich, wie alles mit allem zusammenhängt.

Das ist die Idee hinter diesem Buch, das gemeinsam von der Liz Mohn Stiftung und der Bertelsmann Stiftung entwickelt wurde. Jeder der 100 Menschen in unserem globalen Dorf steht heute stellvertretend für etwa 80 Millionen reale Erdenbürger:innen. Wenn in einer Statistik steht, dass 36 Prozent der Weltbevölkerung in China und Indien leben, sind es in unserem Buch 36 von 100 Dorfbewohner:innen. Abstrakte Zahlen werden auf diese Weise greifbar.

Wir alle sind Teil dieser Welt und bestimmen über unsere gemeinsame Zukunft. Doch dafür müssen wir die Welt begreifen. Wir müssen verstehen, wie eng wir heute mit Menschen aus Ländern, die weit weg erscheinen, verbunden sind. Und wir müssen verstehen, welche Gemeinsamkeiten, aber auch Unterschiede es weltweit gibt. Denn am Ende leben wir alle in *einer* Welt.

In diesem Sinne wünsche ich Ihnen eine anregende Lektüre.

Liz Mohn
Vorsitzende des Vorstandes der Liz Mohn Stiftung

Dear Readers,

More than eight billion people live on our planet. Written as a number it is an eight with nine zeros: 8,000,000,000. Each of us is one of these people and yet we still find it difficult to relate global population statistics to ourselves. Things look different if we reduce the world's entire population to a global village: If we imagine the world having only 100 inhabitants instead of eight billion, it becomes much clearer how everything is connected to everything else.

That is the idea behind this book, which has been jointly developed by the Liz Mohn Foundation and the Bertelsmann Stiftung. Each of the 100 inhabitants of our global village represents approximately 80 million real people on earth. If, statistically speaking, 36 percent of the world's population lives in China and India, then in our book it's 36 out of the village's 100 residents. With that, abstract figures become more tangible.

We're all part of this world and we all have a say in our shared future. But to have our say, we need to understand the world. We need to comprehend how closely connected we are to people in countries that seem so far away. We also have to understand what we have in common, but what differences exist, too. Ultimately, we all live in *one* world.

With that in mind, I hope you find this book both engaging and insightful.

Liz Mohn
Chairwoman of the Executive Board
Liz Mohn Foundation

Einleitung
Introduction

Die Welt, in der wir leben, ist schwer zu begreifen. Täglich erreicht uns eine Flut von Informationen zu globalen Herausforderungen und Entwicklungen: von Umweltkrisen über Ungleichheiten bis hin zu Kriegen. Es gibt jede Menge Daten über die Lebensrealitäten der Menschen weltweit. Aber verstehen wir die Welt, in der wir leben, überhaupt?

Stellen wir uns unsere Welt doch einmal als Dorf mit 100 Menschen vor. In diesem Dorf spielen Geschichten und dort entfalten sich Konflikte der Welt: Reichtum trifft Armut, Zugang zu Bildung steht fehlenden Chancen auf einen Schulbesuch gegenüber, im Dorf gibt es Frieden und schrecklichen Krieg. Anhand unserer 100 Dorfbewohner:innen lernen wir die Chancen und Herausforderungen verstehen und vor allem die Lage derjenigen, die in ganz anderen Lebensumständen leben als wir selbst. Das ist spannend und es zeigt sich, dass nicht alles schlechter geworden ist auf der Welt – auch wenn es oft so scheint.

Unsere Idee, die Welt als Dorf darzustellen, ist nicht neu. Was dieses Buch besonders macht, sind die Themen, die wir uns anschauen. Es geht nicht nur um Alter, Religion oder Sprache, sondern auch um Themen wie Korruption, Menschenrechte oder auch die Frage, wo frei geforscht werden darf. Statistiken zu diesen Bereichen gibt es viele, doch selten werden Entwicklungen auf die globale Einwohnerzahl umgerechnet. In unserem Dorf funktioniert das so: Wenn 59,9 Prozent der Menschen weltweit ein Smartphone besitzen, dann sind das 60 unserer 100 Dorfbewohner:innen.

Als wir die Daten auf die Weltbevölkerung umgerechnet haben, waren wir selbst immer wieder erstaunt. Schauen wir zum Beispiel auf den Stand der Demokratie weltweit. Wenn wir die Zahl der Staaten heranziehen, halten sich die 91 Demokratien weltweit mit 88 Autokratien fast die Waage. Schauen wir uns aber den Anteil der Menschen an, die in Autokratien und Demokratien leben, entsteht ein anderes Bild: Mehr als zwei Drittel (72 Prozent) der Menschen weltweit leben in Autokratien, nur knapp ein Drittel (28 Prozent) in Demokratien.

Auch geografische Verzerrungen spielen für unser Weltbild eine Rolle. Länder wie Russland oder Kanada sind nach Quadratkilometern riesig und sehen auf Karten auch so aus. Aber sie haben erheblich weniger Einwohner:innen als Staaten wie Bangladesch oder Nigeria, die über deutlich weniger Fläche verfügen. Indem wir auf die Einwohnerzahl blicken und nicht auf die Quadratkilometer, entsteht in diesem Buch ein anderes Bild der Welt.

Unsere Welt ist durch eine enorme Vielfalt geprägt und auch unser Dorf mit seinen 100 Menschen ist äußerst vielfältig. Unterschiedliche Kulturen, Religionen, Sprachen, wirtschaftliche Bedingungen und Lebensweisen machen die

The world we live in is difficult to comprehend. Every day, we're flooded with information on global challenges and developments – from environmental crises and inequality to warfare. There is plenty of data about how people around the globe live, day in and day out. But do we really understand the world we live in?

Let's imagine that our world is a village with 100 inhabitants. Stories are set in this village, and it's where the world's conflicts take place: The rich bump up against the poor, people with access to education coexist alongside those who lack the chance to go to school. There is peace in this village, as well as the horrible reality of war. By looking at our 100 villagers, we can come to understand today's opportunities and challenges and, above all, the situation of those who live in very different circumstances than we do. It's intriguing and it shows that not everything has gotten worse in the world – even if it often seems that way.

Viewing the world as a village is not a new idea. What makes this book special are the topics we examine. They go beyond age, religion and language to include issues such as corruption, human rights and the question of where researchers are free to carry out their work. There are many statistics on these subjects, but the relevant developments are rarely reformulated to reflect the global population. In our village, it works like this: If 59.9 percent of people worldwide own a smartphone, then that corresponds to 60 of our 100 villagers.

As we calculated the figures in terms of the globe's population, we were often surprised ourselves. Let's look, for example, at the state of democracy around the globe. If we consider all the countries on the planet, the 91 democracies are almost equally balanced by the 88 autocracies. But if we look at the number of people living under these two different systems, a different picture emerges: More than two-thirds (72 percent) of people worldwide live in an autocracy, while just under one-third (28 percent) live in a democracy.

Geographical distortions also play a role in how we see the world. Countries such as Russia and Canada are huge in terms of their physical size and look that way on maps. But they have considerably fewer inhabitants than countries such as Bangladesh or Nigeria, which in turn have much less area. By looking at the number of inhabitants instead of square kilometers, this book presents a different image of the world.

Our planet is home to enormous diversity, and our village with its 100 people is extremely diverse as well. Different cultures, religions, languages, economic

verschiedenen Lebensrealitäten unserer Mitmenschen weltweit aus. Das lässt sich etwa am Beispiel Waschmaschinen verdeutlichen. Ihre Zahl steht beispielhaft für die wirtschaftliche Entwicklung der Welt und zeigt zugleich, wie unterschiedlich die Lebensstandards auf unserer Erde sind.

Globale Trends wie Urbanisierung, Klimawandel, Migration und Digitalisierung haben in den vergangenen Jahren tiefgreifende Veränderungen bewirkt. Einige Menschen profitieren von diesen Entwicklungen, anderen geht es schlechter.

Unsere Welt ist heute vernetzter als je zuvor. Wirtschaftlich, politisch, gesellschaftlich, aber auch kulturell sind die Menschen eng miteinander verbunden. Somit können Ereignisse in einem Teil unserer Erde weitreichende Auswirkungen auf weit entfernte Länder und Regionen haben. Klimawandel, Flüchtlingsbewegungen oder auch die Covid-19-Pandemie machen das seit einigen Jahren verstärkt deutlich. Es ist daher für uns alle wichtig, globale Zusammenhänge und Lebensrealitäten zu verstehen.

Das gilt ganz besonders für Deutschland: Kaum ein Land ist wirtschaftlich international so vernetzt. In unserem erdachten Dorf steht eine Person für etwa 80 Millionen Menschen. Dort würde also eine Person aus Deutschland leben. Diese wäre nicht in der Lage, ihre Herausforderungen allein zu lösen. Sie, wie auch Deutschland in der Realität, braucht Partner, um globale Herausforderungen zu meistern.

In diesem Buch beleuchten wir die Unterschiede und verdeutlichen, dass hinter jeder Statistik ein Mensch steht.

Folgende Fragen haben wir uns gestellt:
- Wie sind Reichtum und Armut weltweit verteilt?
- Welchen Zugang haben Menschen zu Bildung – und wie beeinflusst dies ihre Chancen im Leben?
- Wie steht es um die globale Gesundheitsversorgung – und welche gesundheitlichen Herausforderungen bestehen weltweit?
- Wie sind essenzielle Ressourcen wie Wasser, Nahrung und Energie auf der Welt verteilt – und welche Konflikte ergeben sich daraus?
- Wie beeinflussen die globalen Klimaveränderungen die Lebensbedingungen der Menschen – und wer ist am stärksten betroffen?
- In welchen Regierungssystemen leben die Menschen auf der Welt? Welche Rechte können wie viele Menschen genießen? Und welche Rechte werden wie vielen Menschen verwehrt?

Natürlich mussten wir die Realität vereinfachen, um die Welt als Dorf mit 100 Menschen abbilden und komplexe Entwicklungen in wenigen Zahlen darstellen zu können. Aber genau dadurch wird die Realität greifbar. Wir haben nur Daten aus verlässlichen Quellen verwendet, etwa von den Vereinten Nationen, der Weltbank oder der Weltgesundheitsorganisation und von zahlreichen Nichtregierungsorganisationen, die sich mit globalen Fragen auseinandersetzen.

Dieses Buch zeichnet anhand der Welt als Dorf mit 100 Menschen ein Porträt unserer globalen Gemeinschaft. Es zeigt die Herausforderungen auf – genauso wie Möglichkeiten, diese zu bewältigen. Unser Buch ist eine Einladung, darüber nachzudenken, wie wir aktiv eine gerechtere und nachhaltigere Welt gestalten können. Das sind große Aufgaben und für Leser:innen, die mehr wissen möchten, haben wir Hinweise auf weiterführende Quellen aufgenommen.

Nun geht sie los, unsere Reise in das Dorf mit 100 Menschen, die so verschieden sind und leben, wie es auf unserer Welt nun mal ist. Viel Spaß bei der Entdeckungsreise!

Prof. Dr. Daniela Schwarzer
Mitglied des Vorstandes der Bertelsmann Stiftung

conditions and lifestyles make up the different realities of our fellow human beings worldwide. This can be seen in the example of washing machines, whose widespread presence is an indicator of the world's economic development and, at the same time, shows how different living standards can be on our planet.

Global trends like urbanization, climate change, migration and digitalization have brought about far-reaching transformation in recent years. Some people have benefited from these developments, others are worse off.

Our world today is more interdependent than ever before. Economically, politically, socially and culturally, people are closely connected. That means events in one part of the globe can have momentous consequences for distant countries and regions. Climate change, refugee flows and the Covid-19 pandemic have made this increasingly clear in recent years. That's why it's important for all of us to understand global contexts and realities.

This is especially true for Germany, since few other countries have as many international economic ties. In our imaginary village, one inhabitant represents approximately 80 million people. That means there would be one person from Germany in the global village. That person would not be able to tackle the problems they face alone. They, like Germany in the real world, would need partners to overcome global challenges.

In this book, we shed light on the differences and show that there is a person behind every statistic. We've asked ourselves the following questions:
- Where are wealth and poverty present globally?
- What access do people have to education – and how does this affect their chances in life?
- What does health care look like around the globe – and what health challenges exist?
- How are essential resources, such as water, food and energy, distributed around the world – and what conflicts arise as a result?
- How does global climate change affect people's living conditions – and who is impacted most?
- Which systems of government do people live under around the world? Which rights are enjoyed by how many people? And which rights are denied to how many people?

Of course, we've had to simplify reality to depict the world as a village of 100 people and present complex developments with just a few figures. But exactly that is what makes reality tangible. We've only used data from reliable sources, such as the United Nations, the World Bank and the World Health Organization, and from numerous non-governmental organizations that address global issues.

By depicting the world as a village of 100 people, this book paints a portrait of our global community. It shows the challenges we face – as well as possibilities for overcoming them. Our book is an invitation to think about how we can actively shape a more just and more sustainable world. These are major tasks, and for readers who would like to know more, we provide links to sources offering additional in-depth information.

Now it begins – our excursion to the village of 100 people, who are as diverse as the world's inhabitants and who live exactly as they do. Have fun on this journey of discovery!

Prof. Dr. Daniela Schwarzer
Member of the Executive Board
Bertelsmann Stiftung

I Kontinente
Continents

Die Verteilung der Weltbevölkerung auf die einzelnen Kontinente unseres globalen Dorfes ist eindrucksvoll: 59 der 100 Bewohner:innen leben in Asien. Anders formuliert: In Asien leben mehr Menschen als im gesamten Rest der Welt. Die Bevölkerung ist in den vergangenen Jahrhunderten stark gewachsen und dieser Trend wird sich auch in den kommenden Jahrzehnten noch fortsetzen. Doch die demografischen Entwicklungen werden in den Weltregionen unterschiedlich ausfallen. Die Region Asien, deren Bevölkerung in den letzten Dekaden immens gestiegen ist, wird einen relativ geringen Zuwachs haben und Staaten wie China könnten einen demografischen Rückgang erleben. Aber auch in Europa wird die Wende zum negativen demografischen Trend deutlich werden. Die Weltregion mit den relativ höchsten Wachstumszahlen der Bevölkerung wird Afrika sein. Der afrikanische Staat Nigeria könnte bis zum Jahr 2050 die USA als Land mit der drittgrößten Bevölkerung ablösen.

The distribution of the world's population across our global village's continents is impressive, with 59 of its 100 residents coming from Asia. In other words, more people live in Asia than in the rest of the world. The globe's population has grown significantly in recent centuries and this trend will continue in the coming decades. But demographic developments will vary from region to region. Asia, which has grown markedly in recent decades, will have relatively low growth, and countries such as China could even experience a demographic decline. The trend towards negative demographic developments will become evident in Europe as well. The global region with the highest relative population growth will be Africa. Nigeria could replace the United States as the country with the third largest population by 2050.

2022

2050

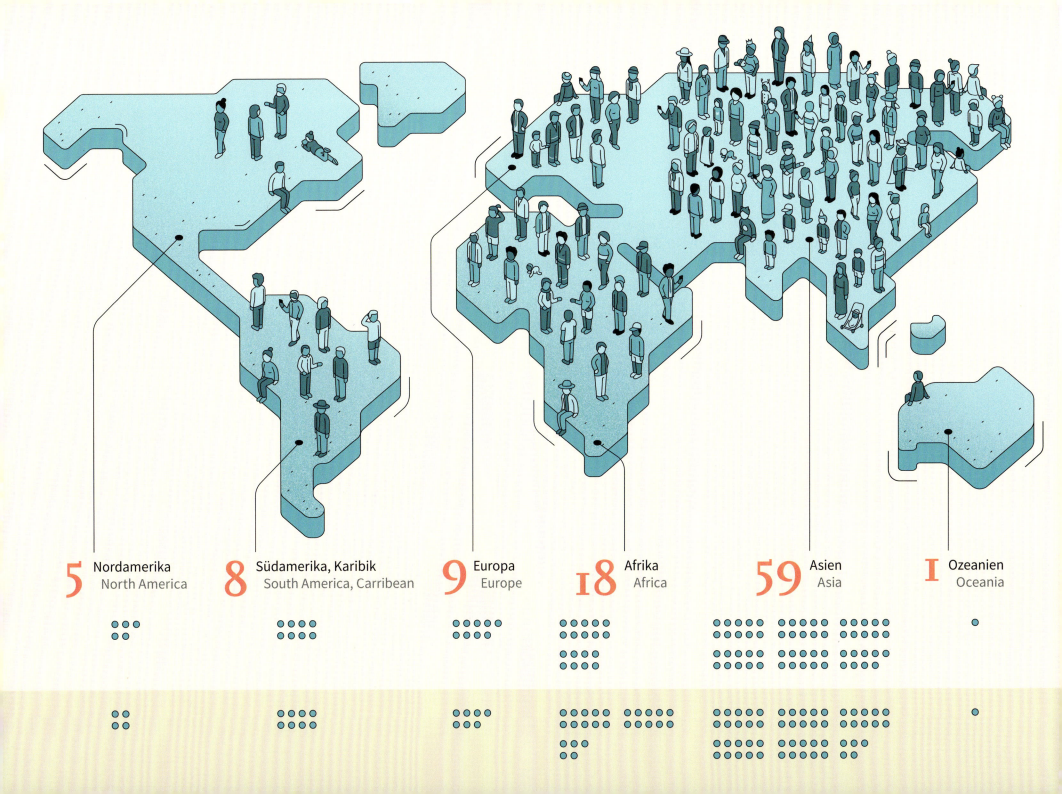

2 Länder
Countries

Wenn wir nicht nur die Kontinente, sondern die einzelnen Länder betrachten, wird deutlich, dass es vor allem zwei asiatische Staaten sind, die einen großen Teil der Weltbevölkerung beheimaten. In den beiden bevölkerungsreichsten Ländern des Planeten – Indien und China – leben in unserem globalen Dorf jeweils 18 Personen. Nachdem China jahrzehntelang das Land mit den meisten Einwohner:innen war, wurde es im Jahr 2023 aufgrund des schnelleren Bevölkerungswachstums von Indien überholt. Die Bevölkerung Indiens wird in den nächsten Dekaden weiter wachsen, während die Bevölkerung Chinas zurückgehen wird. Einige Prognosen gehen davon aus, dass die chinesische Bevölkerung unter eine Milliarde fallen wird. Zum Vergleich: Nur jede:r einhundertste Bewohner:in des Planeten wohnt in Deutschland.

If we look not only at continents, but also at individual countries, it becomes clear that there are two Asian countries in particular that are home to a large part of the world's population: India and China. They are the planet's two most populous countries, and 18 people from each of them live in our global village. After being the most populous country for decades, China was overtaken by India in 2023 due to its faster population growth. India's population will continue to increase over the next few decades, while China's will decline. Some forecasts even suggest that less than one billion people will one day reside in China. In comparison, only one of the 100 inhabitants living in our global village comes from Germany.

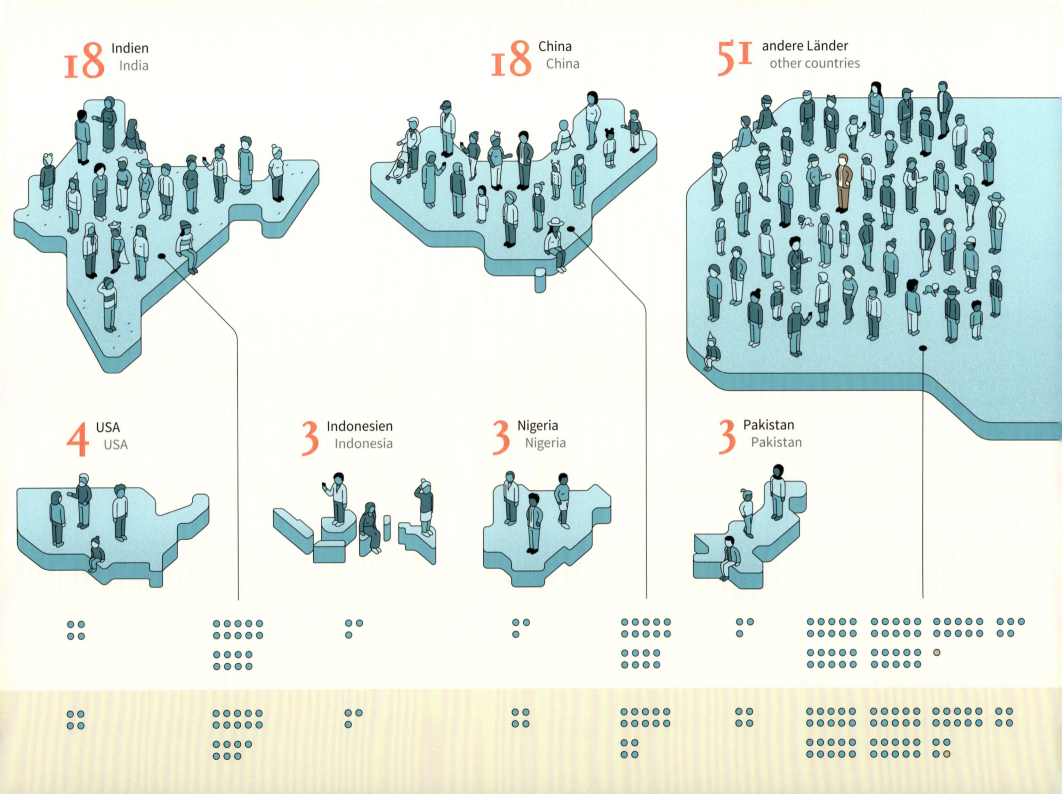

3 Alter
Age

Die Altersstruktur in den unterschiedlichen Weltregionen unterscheidet sich stark. Nirgendwo ist der Gegensatz so groß wie zwischen Europa und Afrika – auch wenn beide Kontinente an der Straße von Gibraltar zwischen Spanien und Marokko nur 14 Kilometer auseinanderliegen. In Europa gibt es mehr Senior:innen als Kinder und Jugendliche (18 Prozent über 64 Jahre, 16 Prozent unter 15 Jahre), während in Afrika die Zahl der Kinder und Jugendlichen die der Älteren bei Weitem übersteigt (drei Prozent über 64 Jahre, 41 Prozent unter 15 Jahre). Nach Berechnungen der Vereinten Nationen (UN) wird sich der Anteil der über 60-Jährigen bis zum Jahr 2050 weltweit auf 21,5 Prozent (oder auf 2,1 Milliarden) erhöhen – heute liegt er zwischen zwölf und 13 Prozent. Der demografische Wandel ist eine große Herausforderung für alternde Gesellschaften wie die deutsche. Immer weniger junge müssen sich um immer mehr ältere Menschen kümmern.

The age structure of the world's population varies greatly from region to region. Nowhere is the contrast as great as between Europe and Africa, even though both continents are only 14 kilometers apart at the Strait of Gibraltar, which separates Spain and Morocco. In Europe, there are more seniors than children and young people (18 percent over 64 years, 16 percent under 15 years), while in Africa the number of children and young people exceeds by far that of older people (3 percent over 64 years, 41 percent under 15 years). According to estimates by the UN, the share of people over 60 will increase to 21.5 percent (or 2.1 billion) by 2050 – today it's between 12 and 13 percent. Demographic change is a major challenge for aging societies like Germany's, where fewer and fewer young people will have to look after more and more older people.

25 bis 14 / up to 14

65 15 bis 64 / 15 to 64

10 65 und älter / 65 and older

4 Muttersprachen
Native languages

Die Muttersprache – oder auch Erstsprache – lernen Menschen im Kindesalter ohne formalen Unterricht in ihrem Umfeld. Mandarin-Chinesisch ist die Sprache mit den meisten Muttersprachler:innen weltweit. In China werden mehrere Sprachen gesprochen, aber Mandarin ist davon die wichtigste. In unserem globalen Dorf mit 100 Einwohner:innen sprechen zwölf von ihnen diese Sprache. Danach folgt Spanisch mit sechs Muttersprachler:innen. Die meisten von ihnen leben in Lateinamerika in unabhängigen Staaten, die früher einmal spanische Kolonien waren. Das prägt die Länder bis heute. Die spanische Sprache und die christliche Religion – beides von den Spaniern ab dem 16. Jahrhundert dort eingeführt – sind für diese Länder charakteristisch.

People learn their mother tongue, or first language, in childhood without any formal instruction. Mandarin Chinese is the language with the most native speakers in the world. Several languages are spoken in China, but Mandarin is the most important. In our global village of 100 people, 12 speak this language. This is followed by Spanish with six native speakers, most of whom are from Latin American countries that were once Spanish colonies. This shapes life in these countries to this day, as the Spanish language and Christian religion – both introduced by the Spanish beginning in the 16th century – are still widespread there.

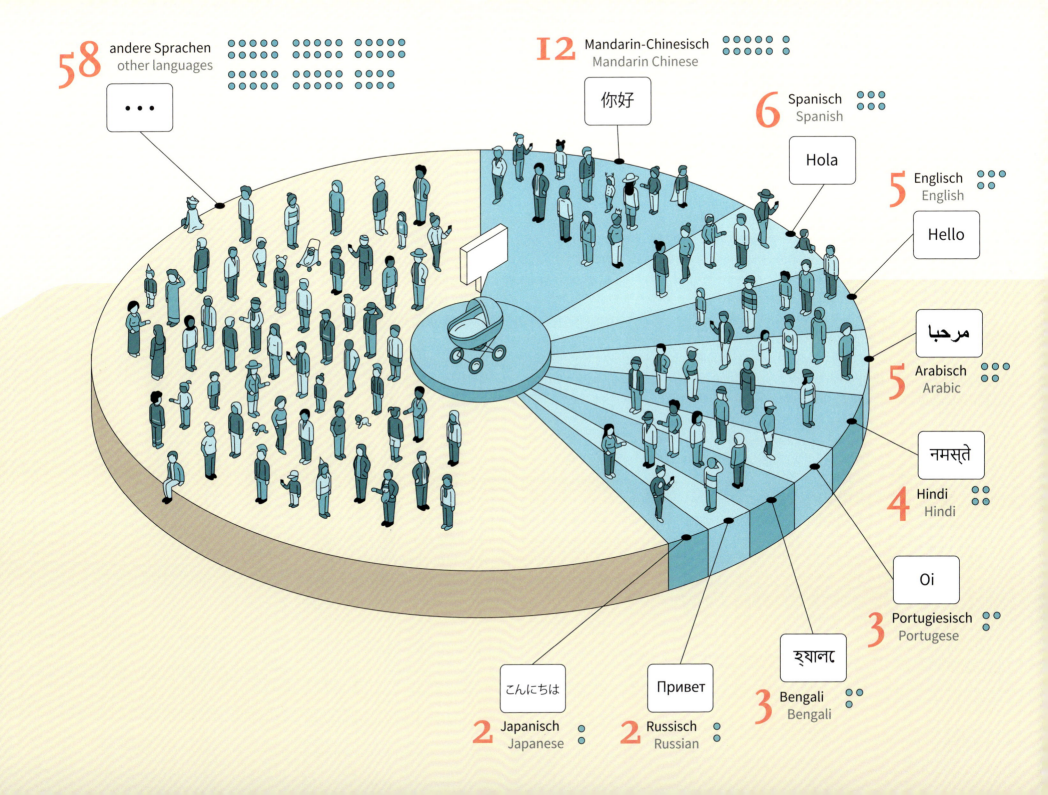

5 Weltsprachen
World languages

Als Muttersprache landet Englisch nur auf Platz drei, aber als gesprochene Weltsprache ist es Spitzenreiter im internationalen Vergleich. Von den 100 Bewohner:innen unseres Dorfes können 19 Englisch sprechen – so viele wie keine andere Sprache. Also können viele Menschen Englisch sprechen, doch die meisten von ihnen haben es als Fremdsprache erlernt. Das bedeutet, dass Englisch die meistgelernte Fremdsprache der Welt ist, aber andere Sprachen – nämlich Mandarin und Spanisch – mehr Muttersprachler:innen haben. Urdu wird von knapp drei Prozent der Menschen gesprochen – vor allem in Pakistan und einigen Regionen Indiens. Neben Spanisch wurden auch die europäischen Sprachen Englisch, Französisch und Portugiesisch durch die Kolonialisierung in weit entfernte Weltregionen gebracht. Diese Sprachen werden dort noch heute gesprochen, zum Beispiel Englisch in Indien, Französisch in vielen westafrikanischen Staaten und Portugiesisch in Brasilien.

As a native language, English only comes in third place internationally, but as a language spoken by people around the world, it ranks first. Of the 100 residents of our village, 19 speak English – more than any other language – even though most of them learned it as a foreign language. In other words, English is the most acquired foreign language in the world, but others, namely Mandarin and Spanish, have more native speakers. Urdu is spoken by almost 3 percent of the globe's population – especially in Pakistan and some parts of India. Spanish is not the only European language that was brought to distant parts of the world through colonialization; so were English, French and Portuguese. Today, these languages are still spoken where they were introduced back then, for example English in India, French in Africa and Portuguese in Brazil.

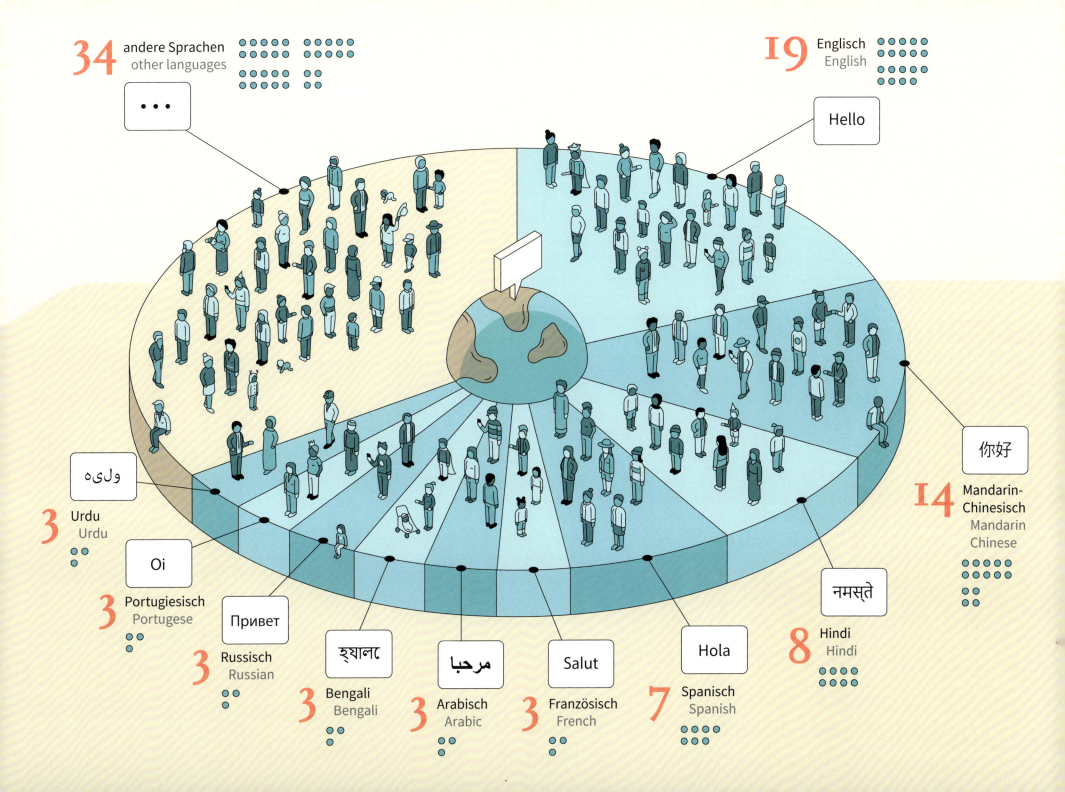

6 Religion
Religion

Glauben ist eine sehr persönliche Sache. Ob und, wenn ja, welchen Gott wir als Teil unseres Lebens sehen, entscheidet jede:r für sich. Glauben und Kultur beeinflussen sich gegenseitig. In Deutschland verlieren die christlichen Kirchen seit Jahren Mitglieder. Und die Mitgliedszahlen der katholischen und der evangelischen Kirche unterscheiden sich in den einzelnen Regionen Deutschlands stark. Doch bilden Christ:innen weltweit noch immer die größte Glaubensgemeinschaft. Nach den Muslim:innen folgen auf dem dritten Platz bereits die Menschen, die sich keiner Religion (mehr) zugehörig fühlen. Vor allem in Regionen mit niedriger Geburtenrate ist der Bevölkerungsanteil derjenigen groß, die sich als nicht gläubig bezeichnen. In Weltregionen mit hohen Geburtenraten ist die Zugehörigkeit zu Religionsgemeinschaften dagegen ausgeprägter. Der größte Zuwachs für christliche und muslimische Glaubensgemeinschaften wird in Subsahara-Afrika erwartet.

Faith is a very personal thing. Everyone decides individually whether God – and, if so, which God – is part of their lives. Faith and culture influence and reinforce each other. In Germany, Christian churches have been losing members for years, and the number of members that the Catholic and Protestant Churches still have varies greatly across the country's regions. However, Christians continue to make up the largest religious community worldwide, followed by Muslims. In third place are people who no longer feel they belong to any religion. The share of people who describe themselves as non-believers is especially large in global regions with low birth rates. In those with high birth rates, membership in religious communities is more pronounced. The greatest growth for Christian and Muslim religious communities is expected in sub-Saharan Africa.

Deutschland / Germany

- **44** keine Religion / not religious
- **25** Katholiken / Catholics
- **23** Protestanten / Protestants
- **4** Muslime / Muslims
- **2** Christlich-Orthodoxe / Christian Orthodox
- **2** andere Religionen / other religions

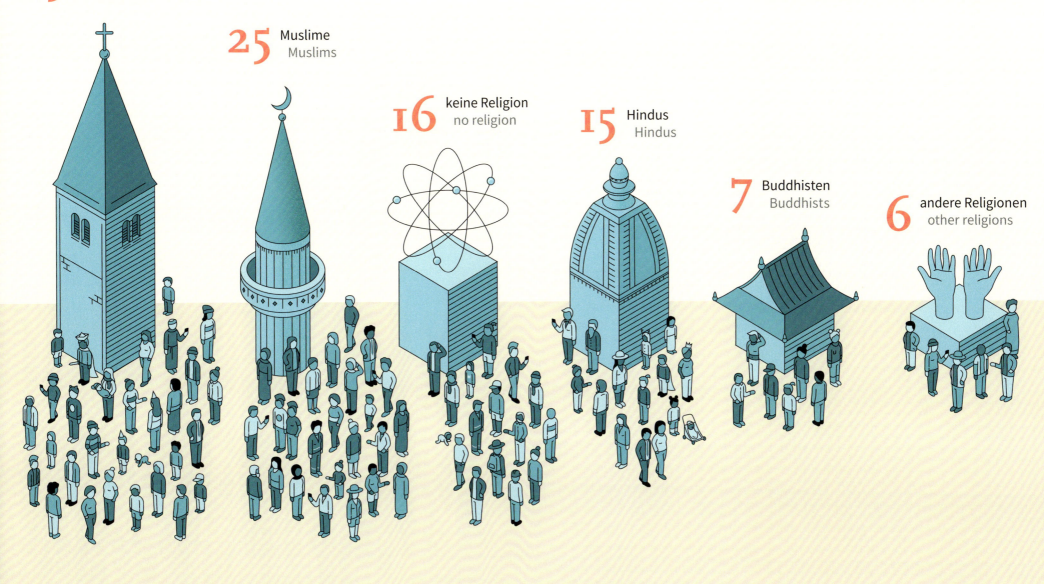

7 Wohnort
Place of residence

Die Städte wachsen. Das ist die eindeutige Botschaft dieser Zahlen. 1960 haben noch zwei Drittel der Menschen auf dem Land gelebt, heute sind es weniger als die Hälfte. Millionenmetropolen und Großstädte ziehen weltweit Menschen an – dieser Trend zeigt sich vor allem in Schwellen- und Entwicklungsländern. Dafür gibt es viele Gründe. Oft sind es Jobmöglichkeiten und die bessere Infrastruktur, die neue Bewohner:innen anziehen. Mit der wachsenden Urbanisierung folgen aber auch zahlreiche Herausforderungen für die Umwelt, das Zusammenleben und die Gesundheitssysteme. Große Probleme in den Bereichen Wasserversorgung, Sanitäranlagen, Energieversorgung und Wohnraum bleiben vielerorts bestehen.

The world's cities are growing. That is the clear message provided by our numbers. In 1960, two-thirds of the global population lived in rural areas – today it's less than half. Metropolitan areas and large cities are attracting people worldwide, a trend that can be seen primarily in emerging and developing countries. There are many reasons for this. Job opportunities and better infrastructure are often the factors that attract new inhabitants. However, growing urbanization also presents numerous challenges for the environment, health systems and communal life. Major problems related to the water supply, sanitation, energy and housing continue to exist in many places.

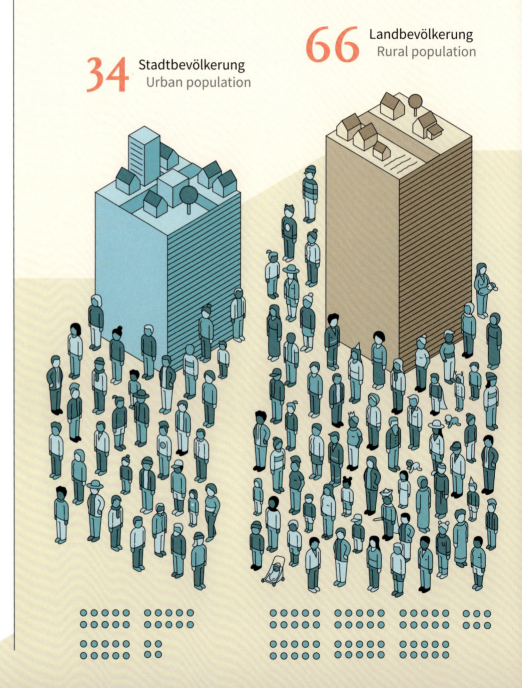

1960

34 Stadtbevölkerung / Urban population

66 Landbevölkerung / Rural population

8 Armenviertel
Slums

Mit der Urbanisierung gehen auch wachsende Armenviertel einher. In den Slums, Favelas oder auch Elendsviertel genannten Siedlungen leben Menschen mit wenig Geld dicht beieinander. Diese Viertel wachsen vor allem dann, wenn viele Menschen in großen Städten leben möchten, ohne dass es für sie dort bezahlbaren Wohnraum gibt. In den Slums gibt es kaum lebensnotwendige Infrastruktur. Die provisorischen Bauten verfügen über kein funktionierendes Stromnetz; auch eine Versorgung mit sauberem Wasser oder eine Kanalisation gibt es dort meist nicht. Zudem fehlen öffentliche Dienstleistungen wie die Müllabfuhr oder ein Personennahverkehr. Armut, Krankheit und Diskriminierung sind im Alltag oft die Folgen. Der Anteil der Slumbewohner:innen steigt in den kommenden Jahrzehnten voraussichtlich auf knapp ein Drittel der Weltbevölkerung.

Urbanization is also accompanied by the growth of slums, also known as favelas. Slums are densely populated urban areas where people with little money live. These neighborhoods often arise when many people want to live in big cities that lack affordable housing. Slums offer little of the infrastructure necessary for a decent life. The temporary dwellings are not served by a functioning electricity network, and there is usually no supply of clean water and no sewer system. In addition, there are no public services such as garbage collection or local public transport. Poverty, illness and discrimination are often the everyday consequences. The number of people living in slums is expected to rise to almost a third of the world's population in the coming decades.

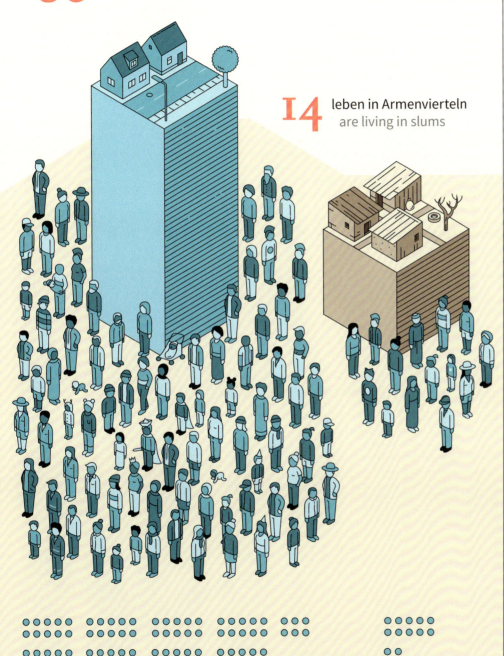
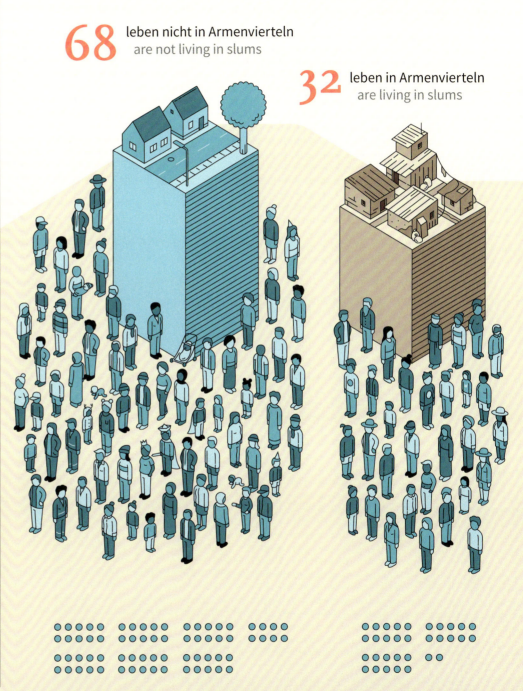

9 Analphabetismus
Illiteracy

Lesen und schreiben zu können, ist wichtig für ein selbstbestimmtes Leben. Denn im beruflichen und privaten Alltag sind Texte allgegenwärtig. Weltweit gehen immer noch weniger Mädchen als Jungen zur Schule. Daher gibt es unter den Menschen, die nicht lesen und schreiben können, weltweit mehr Frauen (17 Prozent Analphabetenquote) als Männer (zehn Prozent). In Deutschland ist es umgekehrt: Hierzulande sind mehr Männer als Frauen betroffen. Die Entwicklung über die vergangenen Jahrzehnte ist jedoch positiv. Weltweit können heute viel mehr Menschen lesen und schreiben als früher. 1990 lag die weltweite Analphabetenquote noch bei mehr als 25 Prozent; 2022 liegt sie bei 13 Prozent. Um auf die Situation der Menschen aufmerksam zu machen, die nicht richtig lesen und schreiben können, gibt es den Weltalphabetisierungstag, der jedes Jahr am 8. September begangen wird.

Being able to read and write is essential if a person is to lead a self-determined life. After all, written texts are an important part of daily existence, in both professional and private contexts. Worldwide, fewer girls than boys go to school, so there are more women (17 percent illiteracy rate) than men (10 percent) who cannot read or write. It's the other way around in Germany, where more men than women are illiterate. The trend over the past few decades, however, has been positive, since many more people worldwide can now read and write. In 1990, the global illiteracy rate was over 25 percent; in 2022, it was 13 percent. Held every year on September 8, World Literacy Day draws attention to the situation of people unable to read or write.

Deutschland / Germany

88 Alphabeten are literate

12 Analphabeten are illiterate

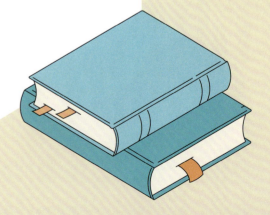

87 sind Alphabeten
are literate

13 sind Analphabeten
are illiterate

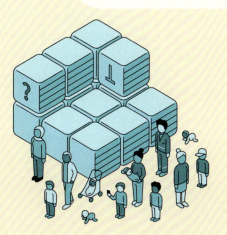

10 Bildung
Education

Lesen und schreiben lernen wir normalerweise in der Schule. Aber in vielen Ländern ist es ein Privileg, überhaupt in die Schule gehen oder später studieren zu können. Und auch eine weiterführende Schule zu besuchen, ist oft schwierig. Zehn von unseren 100 Dorfbewohner:innen haben noch nicht einmal die Möglichkeit, zur Grundschule zu gehen. Unter ihnen finden sich besonders viele Analphabet:innen. Schulen gibt es schon seit mehreren Tausend Jahren als Orte der Bildung. Damals besuchten nur Kinder aus wohlhabenden Familien die Schule. Heutzutage herrscht in Ländern wie Deutschland Schulpflicht. Das heißt, Kinder müssen bis zu einem gewissen Alter den Unterricht besuchen – unabhängig davon, ob sie Lust haben oder nicht.

Reading and writing are usually learned at school. But in many countries, going to school or, later, university is a privilege. Attending secondary school is also often a problem. In fact, 10 of our 100 villagers don't even have the opportunity to go to primary school, which means many of those 10 are illiterate. Schools have existed for thousands of years to educate the young, although, in the past, only children from wealthy families could attend. Nowadays, in countries like Germany, education is compulsory, which means that children must go to school up to a certain age – whether they want to or not.

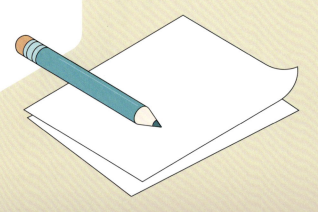

90 Grundschule / Primary education

66 Sekundarschule / Secondary education

39 Hochschule / Tertiary education

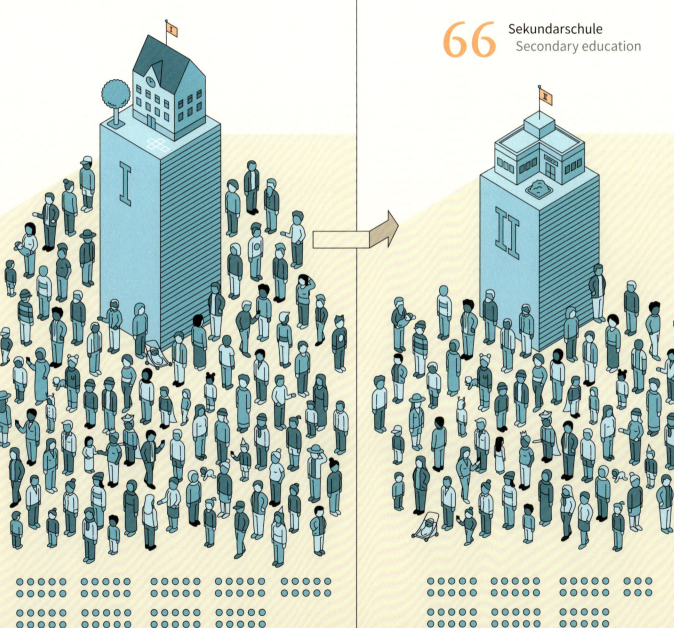

II Arbeit
Work

Auf der ganzen Welt gehen Menschen arbeiten. So verdienen sie Geld, um sich und ihre Familien zu finanzieren. Von unseren 100 Dorfbewohner:innen sind 45 erwerbstätig; die anderen 55 sind vor allem Kinder, Jugendliche sowie Senior:innen. In Deutschland arbeiten sogar mehr als die Hälfte, nämlich 55 Prozent. Die Jobs kann man in drei traditionelle Sektoren aufteilen: Landwirtschaft, Industrie und Dienstleistungen. Früher haben viele Menschen in der Landwirtschaft gearbeitet – 1991 waren es weltweit noch 45 Prozent –, heute sind es nur noch zwölf Prozent. Das liegt vor allem daran, dass viele Arbeitsschritte von Maschinen übernommen wurden, um effizienter und produktiver zu werden. Somit werden weniger Menschen für eine größere landwirtschaftliche Produktion benötigt. Leider gibt es in vielen Ländern noch immer Kinderarbeit. Laut Schätzungen müssen weltweit 160 Millionen Kinder arbeiten. Diese haben davon oft lange körperliche und psychische Schäden.

All over the world, people go to work in order to earn money and support themselves and their families. Of our 100 villagers, 45 are employed, while the other 55 are mainly children, young people and seniors. In Germany, more than half of all people in the country work – 55 percent. In general, jobs can be divided into three traditional sectors: agriculture, industry and services. Many people used to work in agriculture – 45 percent worldwide in 1991 – but today the figure is only 12 percent. This is mainly because machines have taken over many processes, making them more efficient and effective. Consequently, fewer people are needed to produce more agricultural goods. Unfortunately, child labor still exists in many countries: An estimated 160 million children have to work worldwide. Long-term physical and psychological damage is often the result.

Deutschland / Germany

45 nicht arbeitende Personen / Non-working people

55 arbeitende Personen / Working people

41 Dienstleistungen / Services

1 Landwirtschaft / Agriculture

13 Industrie / Industry

55 nicht arbeitende Personen
Non-working people

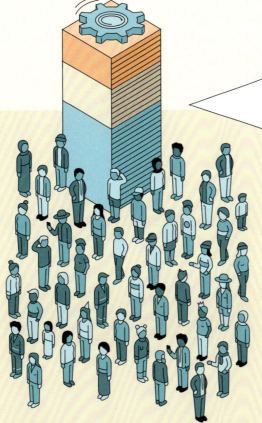

45 arbeitende Personen
Working people

Arbeitssektoren
Labor sectors

22 Dienstleistungen
Services

12 Landwirtschaft
Agriculture

11 Industrie
Industry

12 Einkommen
Income

Geld ist in modernen Gesellschaften lebensnotwendig. Damit zahlen wir Trinkwasser, Lebensmittel, Miete, Kleidung und viele andere Dinge, die wir zum Leben brauchen. Dabei ist die Höhe des Einkommens, also wie viel Geld man verdient, in den Ländern sehr unterschiedlich. Aber auch die Lebenshaltungskosten sind in manchen Ländern höher, in anderen niedriger. Daher kann man mit einem bestimmten Betrag in einem Land gut leben, in einem anderen aber nicht. Und selbst innerhalb eines Landes gibt es große Preisunterschiede zwischen den Regionen, Städten und Vierteln. Trotzdem ist es interessant zu sehen, wie viel die Menschen auf der Welt verdienen. In unserem globalen Dorf haben nur 16 Personen ein Einkommen von mindestens 13.846 US-Dollar im Jahr. Das bedeutet, dass die ärmere Hälfte der Dorfbewohner:innen von wenigen Dollar pro Tag lebt.

Money is fundamental in a modern society. We use it to pay for food and water, as well as for rent, clothing and many of the other things we need to live. The level of income – that is, how much money people earn – varies from country to country. However, the cost of living is higher in some countries and lower in others, which is why it's possible to live well on a certain amount in one place, but not in another. Even within a country, prices can differ widely between regions, cities and neighborhoods. Still, it's interesting to see how much people around the world earn. In our global village, only 16 people have incomes of at least $13,846 a year. This means that the poorer half of the villagers live on a few dollars a day.

13 Vermögen
Assets

Zum Vermögen einer Person zählt ihr gesamtes Eigentum. Geld auf dem Konto, Haus, Auto, aber auch Aktien oder andere Besitztümer, die einen Wert haben. Wenn man alles zusammenrechnet, was man als erwachsener Mensch hat, kommt man schnell auf eine höhere Summe als gedacht – zumindest in den wohlhabenderen Ländern der Welt. Das gilt aber nicht für die Mehrheit unserer globalen Dorfbewohner:innen. Über die Hälfte von ihnen besitzt weniger als 10.000 US-Dollar, aber immerhin eine:r von den 100 Personen ist Millionär:in. Das Vermögen deutlich zu erhöhen, ist für die meisten Menschen schwierig – oft bleiben sie ihr ganzes Leben in derselben (niedrigen) Vermögensgruppe.

A person's assets are everything they own: bank accounts, house, car, stocks and any other valuable possessions. If you add up everything, the total is generally more than what you might have originally thought – at least in the world's wealthier countries. But this is not true for the majority of our global villagers. More than half have less than $10,000 in assets – although at least one of the village's 100 inhabitants is a millionaire. Significantly increasing assets is difficult, and most people stay in the same (low) wealth group their entire lives.

53 Weniger als $10.000 / less than $10,000

34 $10.000 bis $100.000 / $10,000 to $100,000

12 $100.001 bis $1 Mio. / $100,001 to $1 mill.

1 Mehr als $1 Mio. / more than $1 mill.

14 Bankkonto
Bank account

Ein Bankkonto zu haben, ist wichtig, um viele alltägliche Dinge regeln zu können. Der Arbeitgeber überweist das Gehalt dorthin, die Miete wird davon abgebucht und man kann Geld für größere Anschaffungen oder den nächsten Urlaub sparen. Das klassische Konto bei der Bankfiliale wird dabei immer mehr durch digitale Lösungen ersetzt. Apps auf dem Smartphone, über die sich alle Finanzgeschäfte regeln lassen, haben gerade dort Erfolg, wo es bislang oft kein großes Filialnetz der Banken gibt. So nutzt in Indien, dem bevölkerungsreichsten Land der Welt, knapp ein Drittel der Haushalte digitale Zahlungsmöglichkeiten, denn ein Smartphone haben dort viele Menschen – aber nur ein Teil von ihnen verfügte zuvor über ein klassisches Bankkonto.

Having a bank account is important for managing many aspects of daily life. Your employer transfers your salary to it, it's where the money comes from to pay your rent, and what you use to save for larger purchases or your next vacation. The classic bank account is increasingly being replaced by digital solutions. Smartphone apps that can handle all sorts of financial transactions have proven particularly popular in places where banking networks have not usually been present. In India, the most populous country in the world, almost one-third of the country's households use digital payment options because many people there have a smartphone – even though only some of them previously had a traditional bank account.

76 haben ein Bankkonto
have a bank account

24 haben kein Bankkonto
have no bank account

15 Krankenversicherung
Health insurance

Wenn man krank wird, geht man zum Arzt oder zur Ärztin. Wenn es etwas Schlimmeres ist oder man einen Unfall hatte, kommt man ins Krankenhaus. Für uns ist es normal, dass die Krankenkasse die Kosten dafür übernimmt. Das ist wichtig, denn bei längeren Krankheiten oder Operationen kommen schnell mehrere Tausend Euro zusammen. Damit diese schlecht vorherzusehenden Kosten nicht zu einem ernsten Problem für die Patient:innen werden, ist es in Deutschland gesetzliche Pflicht, eine Krankenversicherung zu haben. Von unseren 100 Dorfbewohner:innen sind mehr als die Hälfte nicht vollkommen geschützt durch eine Krankenversicherung und 13 haben finanzielle Schwierigkeiten aufgrund dieser Situation. Für weitere 13 der 100 Bewohner:innen haben die Behandlungskosten sogar katastrophale finanzielle Konsequenzen.

If you get sick, you go to the doctor. If it's something serious or you've had an accident, you go to the hospital. For people in Germany, it's normal that the costs are covered by health insurance. This is important because long-term illnesses or operations can quickly add up to several thousand euros. To ensure that these difficult-to-predict costs do not become a serious problem, everyone in Germany is required by law to have health insurance. Of our 100 villagers, more than half are not fully covered by health insurance, and 13 experience financial difficulties as a result. For another 13 of the 100, the cost of treatment even has catastrophic economic consequences.

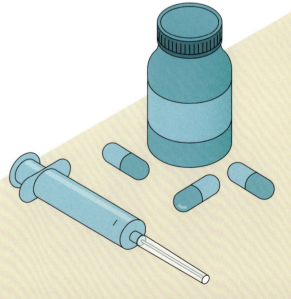

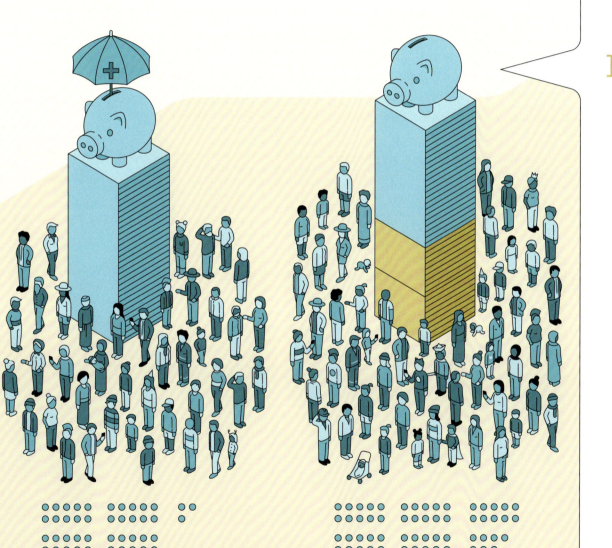

43 sind durch eine Kranken-versicherung geschützt
are covered by health insurance

57 sind nicht vollkommen durch eine Krankenversicherung geschützt
are not fully covered by health insurance

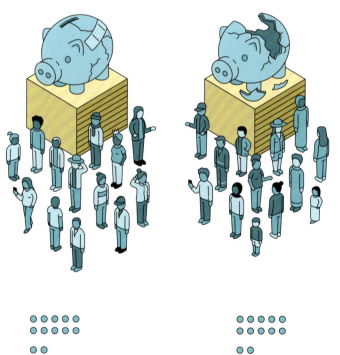

13 sind in finanziellen Schwierigkeiten
experience financial hardship

13 katastrophale Kosten
face catastrophic costs

16 Psychische Gesundheit
Mental health

Die Gesundheit eines Menschen umfasst nicht nur seinen Körper, sondern auch seinen Geist. Es gibt viele verschiedene psychische Störungen und Krankheiten, unter denen die Betroffenen leiden und die sich auf das Denken, Fühlen und Handeln auswirken. Zu den häufigsten Krankheiten zählen Depressionen, Alkoholsucht und Angststörungen. Bei Letzteren haben die Betroffenen im Alltag so starke Ängste, dass ihr Leben beeinträchtigt wird. Von Angststörungen sind weltweit schätzungsweise auch 58 Millionen Kinder und Jugendliche betroffen. Zudem leben etwa 23 Millionen Kinder und Jugendliche weltweit mit Depressionen. Man spricht von dieser Krankheit, wenn traurige Gefühle und negative Gedanken das gesamte Leben bestimmen. Weitere Erkrankungsbilder sind die posttraumatischen Belastungsstörungen, Schizophrenie, Essstörungen, Verhaltensstörungen und dissoziale Störungen sowie Neuroentwicklungsstörungen. Die Daten zur Häufigkeit der Krankheitsbilder sind nur eine Momentaufnahme. Nach Schätzung von neuen großen Studien wird jeder zweite Mensch im Lauf seines Lebens psychische Erkrankungen entwickeln.

A person's health includes not only their body, but also their mind. There are many different mental disorders that cause people to suffer and that have direct consequences for how they think, feel and act. The most common mental illnesses are depression, alcohol addiction and anxiety disorders. People experiencing the latter have such strong fears in everyday situations that they have trouble living their lives. It is estimated that 58 million children and young people worldwide are affected by anxiety disorders. In addition, some 23 million children and young people live with depression, which occurs when sad feelings and negative thoughts overshadow a person's entire life. Other mental illnesses include post-traumatic stress disorder, schizophrenia, eating disorders, disruptive behavioral disorders, antisocial disorders and neurodevelopmental disorders. The data on the frequency of the clinical pictures are only a snapshot. According to estimates from new major studies, one in two people will develop a mental illness in the course of their lives.

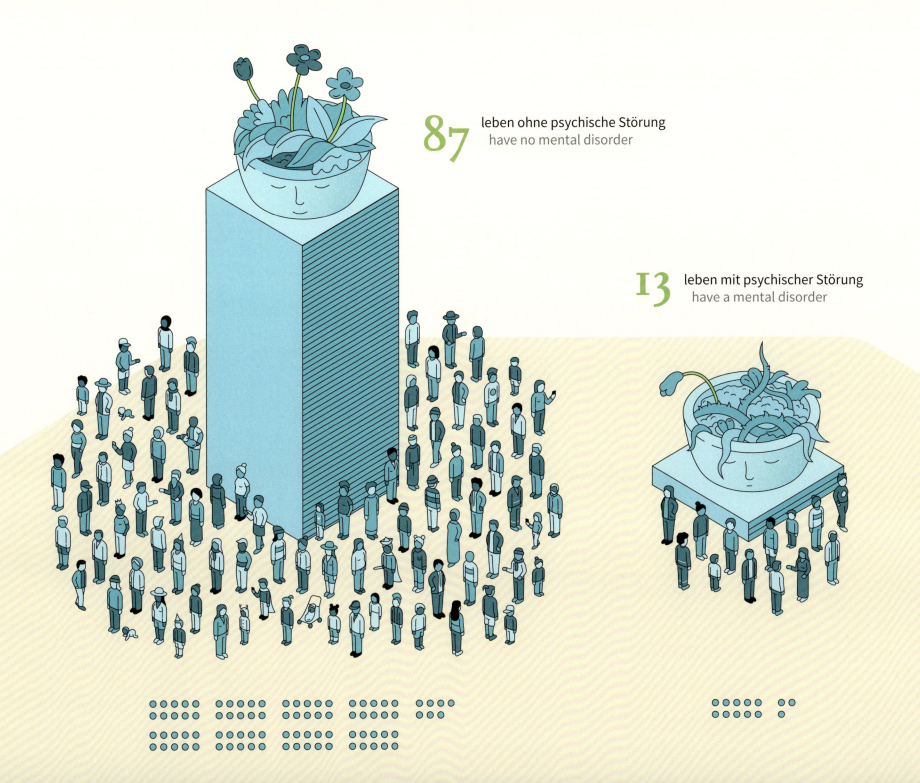

17 Fleischkonsum
Meat consumption

78 der 100 Dorfbewohner:innen ernähren sich von Fleisch. Sie essen regelmäßig Fleisch oder fleischhaltige Gerichte. Auf der anderen Seite ernähren sich 22 der 100 Dorfbewohner:innen fleischlos, also ausschließlich durch vegetarische oder vegane Gerichte – fast alle davon jedoch nicht aus Überzeugung, sondern weil sie sich Fleisch als Nahrungsmittel nicht leisten können. Ein Grund dafür, dass die große Mehrheit der Menschen Fleisch isst, sind die über Jahrhunderte entstandenen Traditionen und Esskulturen. Entsprechend wurde die Fleischproduktion in vielen wohlhabenden Staaten institutionalisiert und industrialisiert. In Deutschland führte dies über Dekaden zu einem großen Angebot für die Bevölkerung unabhängig von ihren Einkommen. Trotzdem bleibt die Produktion von Fleisch ressourcenintensiv. Erst in den letzten Jahren geben immer mehr Menschen in Industrieländern an, sich vegetarisch oder vegan zu ernähren.

Of our 100 villagers, 78 eat meat. They consume it, or dishes containing it, on a regular basis. Conversely, 22 of the 100 have a meat-free diet, meaning they eat exclusively vegetarian or vegan dishes. Almost all of them, however, don't do this out of conviction, but because they can't afford to eat meat. The traditions and food cultures that have developed over the centuries are one reason why the vast majority of people consume meat. In addition, meat production has been institutionalized and industrialized in many wealthy countries. In Germany, this means that people have had a wide range of options for consuming meat for decades, regardless of their income. Nevertheless, meat production remains resource-intensive. Only in recent years have more and more people in industrialized countries chosen to follow a vegetarian or vegan diet.

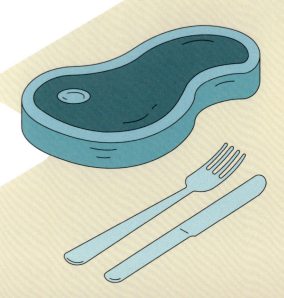

Deutschland / Germany

92 essen Fleisch / consume meat

8 essen kein Fleisch / do not consume meat

78 essen Fleisch
consume meat

22 essen kein Fleisch
do not consume meat

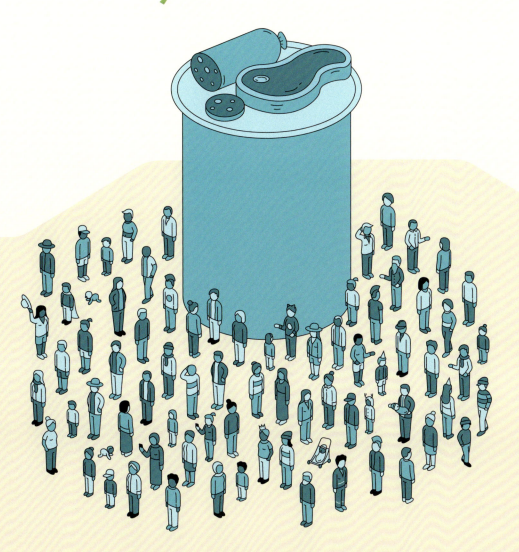
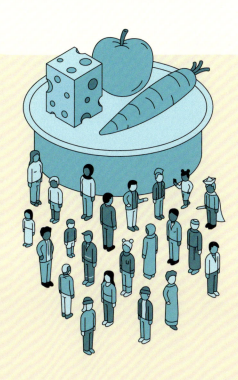

18 Laktoseintoleranz
Lactose intolerance

Joghurt, Käse, Quark, Butter, Sahne: Milch und Milchprodukte sind weltweit als Nahrungsmittel in großer Vielfalt verbreitet. Allerdings kann der Genuss dieser Produkte zu Problemen mit der Verdauung führen. Das passiert, wenn der Laktose genannte Milchzucker vom Körper nicht oder nicht komplett abgebaut wird. Dann bekommen die sogenannten laktoseintoleranten Menschen Bauchschmerzen, Krämpfe, Blähungen oder Durchfall. Meistens ist das genetisch bedingt. Weltweit gibt es große Unterschiede bei dem Anteil laktoseintoleranter Menschen. Am häufigsten kommt das Phänomen in Ostasien vor, wo 70 bis 100 Prozent der Bevölkerung betroffen sind – in Nordeuropa dagegen tritt Laktoseintoleranz fast gar nicht auf.

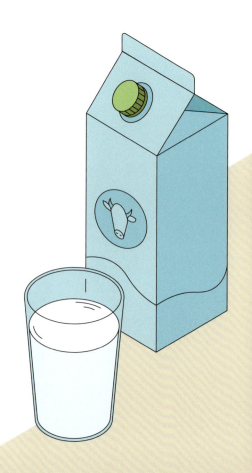

Yoghurt, cheese, butter, cream – milk and milk products are widely consumed all over the world. Eating these products, however, can lead to digestive problems. This happens when the milk sugar called lactose is not adequately broken down by the body. Lactose-intolerant people experience stomach pain, cramps, flatulence or diarrhea. In most cases, the cause is genetic. There are big differences in the number of lactose-intolerant people around the world. The phenomenon occurs most frequently in East Asia, affecting 70 to 100 percent of the population there. In contrast, lactose intolerance is almost never found in Northern Europe.

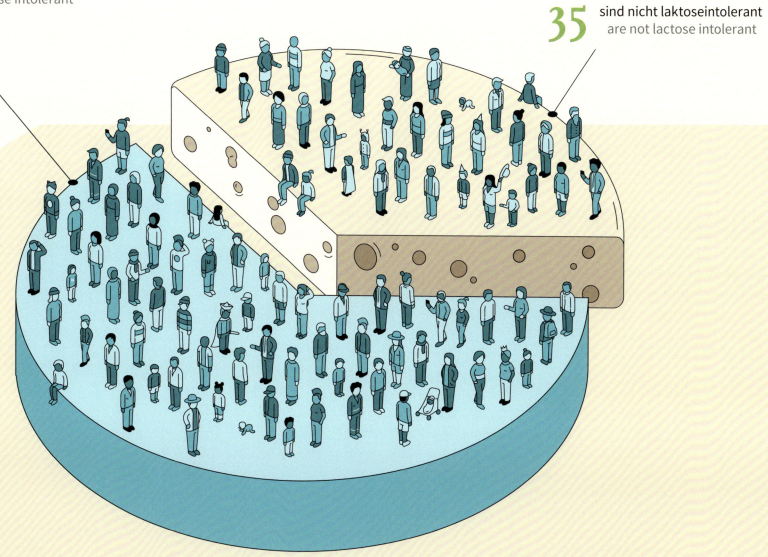

19 Übergewicht
Overweight

Übergewicht betrifft weltweit eine immer größere Zahl von Menschen. In seiner stärksten Ausprägung nennt man es Adipositas. Übergewichtig werden Menschen, wenn sie mehr Energie in Form von Kilokalorien zu sich nehmen, als sie verbrauchen. Das betrifft immer mehr Menschen, denn weltweit bewegen sich viele heute weniger als früher. Besonders Zucker und Fette im Essen tragen zu einer Erhöhung der Kilokalorien und des Körpergewichts bei. Während früher mehr Menschen einer körperlichen Arbeit in der Landwirtschaft oder Industrie nachgingen, haben heutzutage viele einen Schreibtischjob. Auch moderne Transportmittel und der Trend zum Wohnen in Städten führen zu weniger Bewegung und daher zu mehr Übergewicht. In Deutschland ist sogar die Mehrheit der Bevölkerung übergewichtig. Weltweit sterben mehr Menschen an den Folgen von Übergewicht als an den Folgen von Unterernährung. Und in fast jeder Weltregion sind mehr Menschen übergewichtig als untergewichtig. Ausnahmen sind Teilregionen von Subsahara-Afrika und Asien.

Deutschland
Germany

54 sind übergewichtig oder adipös
are overweight or obese

46 sind nicht übergewichtig
are not overweight

Obesity affects an increasing number of people worldwide. In its most severe form it's called adiposity. A person becomes overweight when they consume more calories than they burn, something now true of more and more people worldwide. After all, many people move less today than in the past. Sugar and fats in particular add to the number of calories in food, causing excess body weight. While many people used to have jobs in agriculture or industry that required physical labor, many today work at a desk. More people now live in cities and use modern means of transport, which also results in less exercise and more obesity. In Germany, the majority of the population is overweight. More people worldwide die from obesity than malnutrition. And in almost every global region, more people are overweight than underweight. The exceptions are parts of sub-Saharan Africa and Asia.

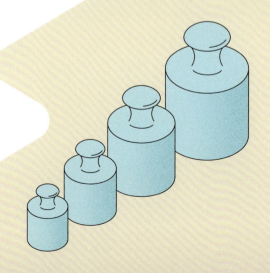

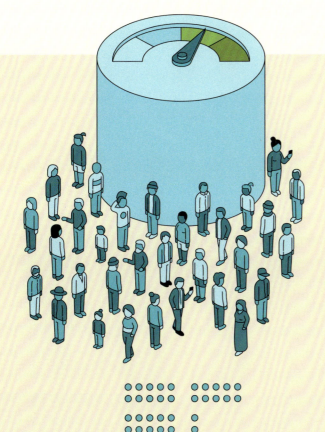

32 sind übergewichtig oder adipös
are overweight or obese

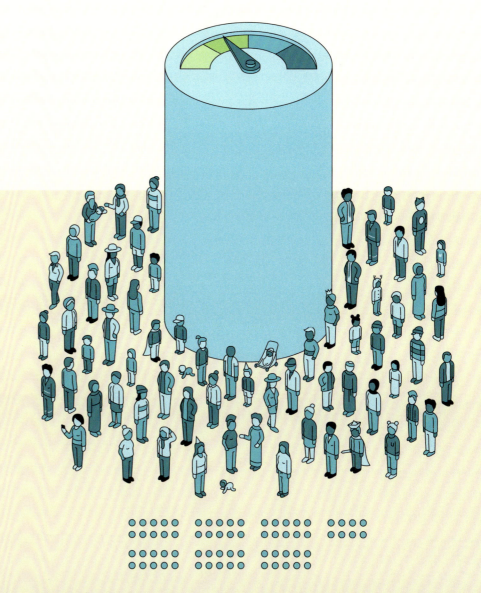

68 sind nicht übergewichtig
are not overweight

20 Unterernährung
Malnutrition

Von Unterernährung spricht man, wenn eine Person regelmäßig nicht genügend Energie in Form von Nahrung zu sich nimmt – sie hat also Hunger. Von unseren 100 Dorfbewohner:innen haben neun Menschen im Alltag nicht genug zu essen. Vor wenigen Jahrzehnten lag der Anteil noch viel höher: 1990 hatten weltweit noch etwa 19 Prozent zu wenig zu essen, sodass fast jeder fünfte Mensch auf der Welt von Unterernährung bedroht war; heute ist es weniger als jeder zehnte. Ein Grund für diesen starken Rückgang sind die Arbeit internationaler Organisationen und die Entwicklung in den betroffenen Ländern. Doch noch heute gibt es in mehreren Ländern Untergewicht und Wachstumshemmungen bei Kindern, obwohl dort kaum Unterernährung vorliegt und die meisten Menschen Zugang zu ausreichend Nahrung haben. Gründe für dieses Untergewicht bei Kindern können Nährstoffmangel durch falsche Ernährung, schlechte Hygienebedingungen oder Krankheiten sein.

Malnutrition occurs when a person does not consume sufficient food on a regular basis. In other words, they go hungry. Of our 100 villagers, nine don't get enough to eat each day. A few decades ago, the number was much higher: about 19 percent in 1990, meaning that almost one person in five was at risk of malnutrition. Today, it is less than one in ten. One reason for this steep decline is the work done by international organizations; another is how at-risk countries have developed. Children continue to be underweight and experience stunted growth in several countries today, although most people there have access to sufficient food and few are at risk of malnutrition. There are a number of factors that can account for this, including a lack of nutrients due to poor nutrition, poor sanitary conditions and diseases.

2023

1990–1992

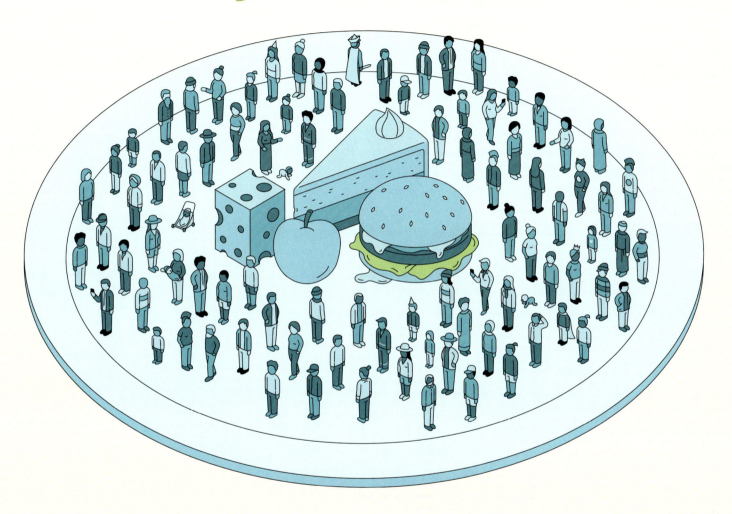

2.1 Toiletten
Toilets

Der Zugang zu einer sauberen Toilette und Sanitäranlage ist für viele Menschen in Europa und im globalen Norden alltäglicher Standard. Ein Leben ohne ein Badezimmer mit fließendem Wasser kann man sich hier gar nicht mehr vorstellen. In Deutschland haben 96 Prozent der Menschen Zugang dazu, also fast alle. Aber noch in der Generation unserer Großeltern oder Urgroßeltern war es nicht überall Standard, ein eigenes Bad in der Wohnung oder im Haus zu haben – oft musste die Toilette mit anderen Familien geteilt werden. Im weltweiten Vergleich wird deutlich, dass auch heutzutage noch viele Menschen keinen sicheren Zugang zu diesen Anlagen haben. 19 unserer 100 Bewohner:innen des globalen Dorfes haben keine Möglichkeit, eine private Toilette zu benutzen und ihre Hände hygienisch mit Wasser zu waschen. Erkrankungen wie Durchfall, Atemwegsinfektionen und Parasitenbefall sind Folgen dieser nicht vorhandenen sicheren Sanitäranlagen. In letzter Konsequenz führt deren weltweites Fehlen jedes Jahr zu mehr als einer Million Todesfällen.

Access to a clean toilet and proper sanitation is the norm for most people in Europe and the Global North. It's hard to imagine life there without a bathroom and running water, something almost everyone in Germany – 96 percent of the population – has access to. Yet just a few generations ago, our grandparents and great-grandparents did not always have a bathroom in their apartment or house – toilets were often shared with other families. A global comparison reveals that, even today, many people still do not have safe access to such facilities, which means 19 of the 100 inhabitants in our global village do not have the possibility of using a private toilet or washing their hands hygienically with water. The absence of well-managed sanitary facilities results in illnesses such as diarrhea, respiratory infections and parasitic infestations. Ultimately, the global lack of safe sanitation causes more than a million deaths each year.

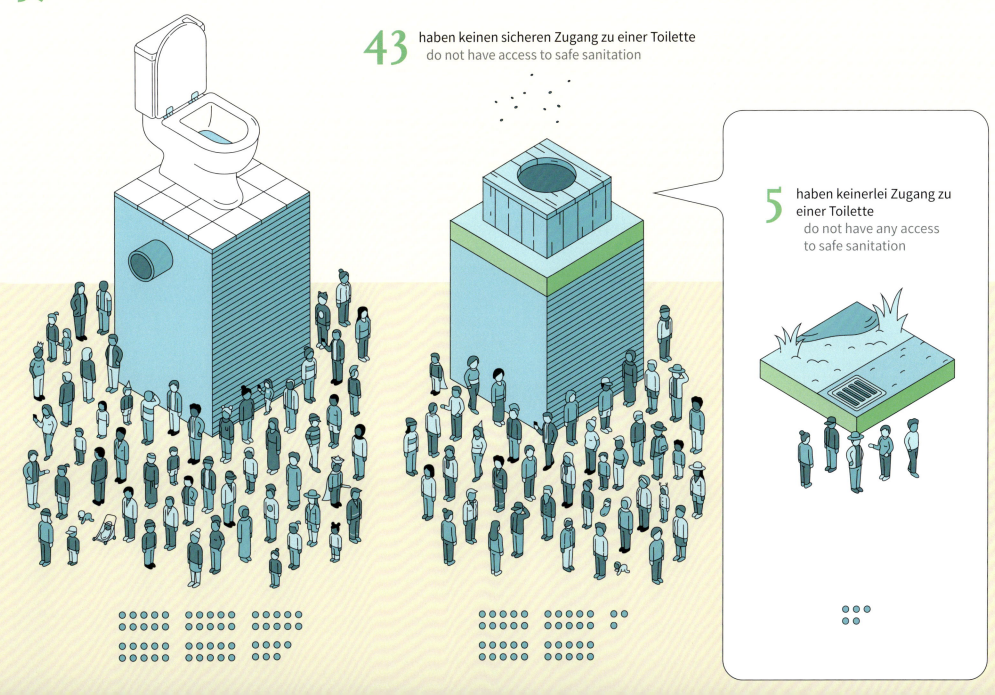

22 Sauberes Trinkwasser
Clean drinking water

Der Zugang zu sauberem Trinkwasser ist wichtig, um einen sorgenfreien Alltag zu haben – so wichtig, dass die Vereinten Nationen ihn sogar zu einem Menschenrecht erklärt haben. In Deutschland und vielen anderen Ländern ist es das Normalste der Welt, jederzeit den Hahn zu öffnen und Trinkwasser in bester Qualität zu bekommen. Das ist aber nicht überall so, obwohl – und das ist die gute Nachricht – sauberes Trinkwasser heutzutage für viel mehr Menschen zugänglich ist als noch vor ein paar Jahrzehnten. Dort, wo es nur wenig Wasser gibt, entstehen oft Konflikte oder sogar Kriege, denn ohne Wasser kann niemand überleben. Der Klimawandel und die dadurch hervorgerufenen Extremwetterereignisse verstärken den Wassermangel in vielen Ländern sogar noch.

Having access to clean drinking water is essential if people are to live untroubled lives. It's so important that the United Nations has even declared it a human right. In Germany and many other countries, opening the tap at any time and getting clean drinking water is the most normal thing in the world. But that's not yet the case everywhere – although, and this is the good news, clean drinking water is now accessible to many more people than it was a few decades ago. Where water is scarce, conflicts often arise, even wars, because no one can survive without water. Extreme weather events caused by the climate change make water shortages even more likely in numerous countries.

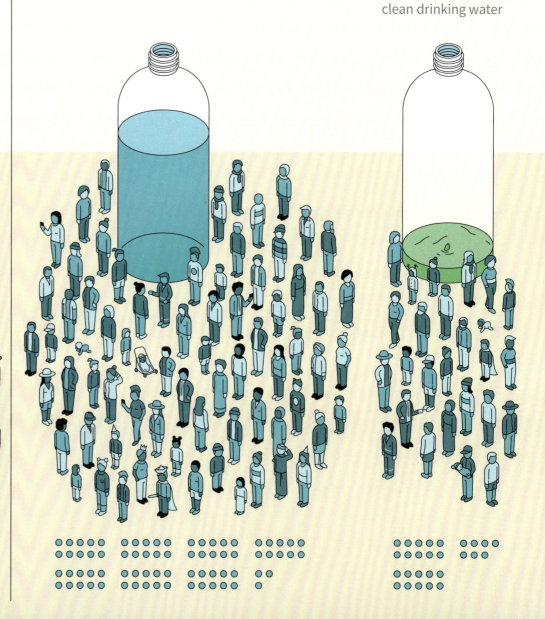

23 Elektrizität
Electricity

Strom aus der Steckdose liefert die notwendige Energie für die Geräte, die wir jeden Tag nutzen: Waschmaschine, Toaster, Smartphone, Fernseher und viele mehr. Dabei müssen sich etliche kleine Teilchen, die sogenannten Elektronen, durch eine Leitung – das Stromkabel – in eine Richtung bewegen, damit die Apparate laufen. Strom ist unsichtbar, aber ohne ihn würden all diese Geräte nicht funktionieren. Das merkt man, wenn es mal einen Stromausfall gibt. In den meisten europäischen Ländern passiert das nicht so häufig, aber in anderen Regionen der Welt kommt es regelmäßig vor. In einer Wohnung oder einem Haus in Deutschland gibt es sehr viele Steckdosen, oft in jedem Raum mindestens eine oder zwei. Doch viele Menschen weltweit müssen ihren Alltag ohne Zugang zu Elektrizität organisieren, denn sie haben bei sich zu Hause nirgends eine direkte Verbindung zu Stromquellen.

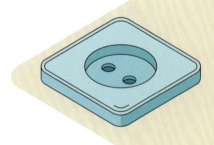

Electricity provides the energy required to power the devices we use every day, such as washing machines, toasters, smartphones and televisions. A constant stream of electrons must move through a conductor such as a cable to create an electric current. And although electricity is invisible, without it none of our gadgets would work – something we quickly notice when there's a power outage. This doesn't happen often in most European countries, but it's a regular occurrence in other parts of the world. Apartments and houses in Germany usually have plenty of outlets, at least one or two in every room. But many people around the globe have to manage without any access to electricity at all, since their homes lack a direct connection to a power source.

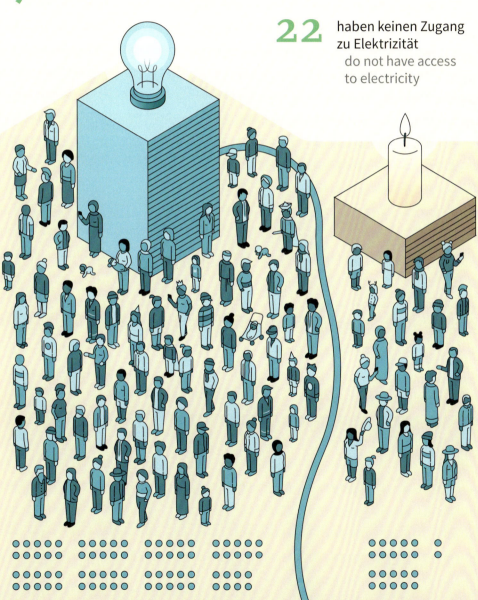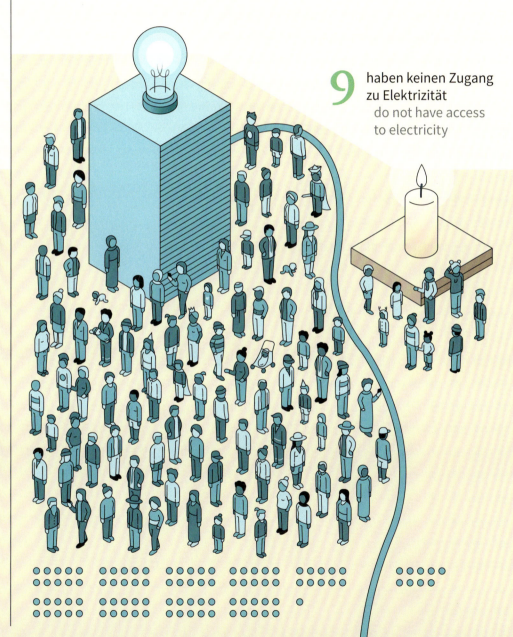

24 Waschmaschinen
Washing machines

Eine Waschmaschine gibt es doch in jedem Haushalt, werden viele sagen. Zumindest für Deutschland und die meisten hoch entwickelten Staaten stimmt das. Aber in fast der Hälfte aller Haushalte weltweit wird per Hand gewaschen. Das ist viel mehr Arbeit für die Person, die sich um die Wäsche kümmert – meistens ist das die Frau. Darum hilft die Waschmaschine oft den Frauen, mehr Zeit für sich, die Familie, den Job oder Hobbys zu haben – und hat seit ihrer Erfindung vor über hundert Jahren einen Siegeszug um die ganze Welt angetreten. In vielen Fällen ist die Waschmaschine das erste elektrische Haushaltsgerät, das angeschafft wird, sobald die Menschen es sich leisten können. Daher lässt sich an der Zahl von Waschmaschinen in einem Land der Wohlstand der Bevölkerung ablesen.

You might think that every household has a washing machine. That's generally true in Germany and most highly developed countries. But in almost half of all households worldwide, washing is done by hand. That means a lot more work for the person doing the laundry – which is often a woman. Consequently, washing machines frequently give women more time for themselves, for their family, for a job or for hobbies – one reason why they have become ubiquitous around the world since being invented over 100 years ago. In many cases, a washing machine is the first electronic household appliance people purchase – as soon as they can afford it. As a result, the number of washing machines present in a country can be seen as an indicator of its level of prosperity.

Deutschland
Germany

96 haben eine Waschmaschine im Haushalt
have a washing machine in their household

4 haben keine Waschmaschine
do not have a washing machine in their household

52 haben eine Waschmaschine im Haushalt
have a washing machine in their household

48 haben keine Waschmaschine
have no washing machine

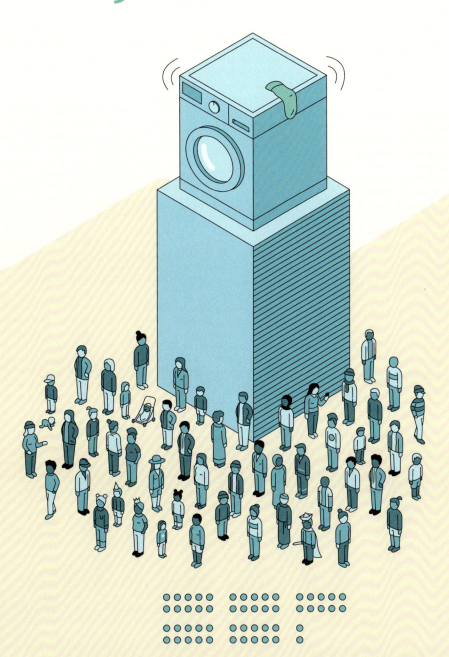

25 Internet
Internet

Das Internet wurde in den USA entwickelt. Zunächst vernetzte es nur wenige Universitäten im Land – heute verbindet es Menschen und Institutionen auf der ganzen Welt miteinander. Ein Internetzugang ist heutzutage wichtiger denn je. Viele Dienstleistungen und die Kommunikation zwischen den Menschen werden durch das Internet erst möglich gemacht. Dadurch erhöht sich auch dessen Nutzen. Regierungen, Geschäfte und Personen setzen ihre Aktivitäten mehr und mehr im Internet um. Dabei lebt jeder dritte Mensch weltweit ohne Internetzugang. In Deutschland haben fast alle Personen in ihrem Haushalt einen Zugang: 92 von 100. Das Internet bietet viele Möglichkeiten, bringt aber auch Probleme mit sich: Kriminalität, Mobbing und Datenlecks sind Themen, die jede:n Nutzer:in betreffen können.

The Internet was developed in the US. At first it connected only a few universities there, today it links people and institutions all over the world. Internet access has become more important than ever. It makes many services possible and allows people to communicate on a broad scale. That, in turn, makes it even more essential as governments, companies and individuals move their activities online. One in three people worldwide has no Internet access at home. In Germany, almost everyone does: 92 people out of 100. The Internet offers many opportunities, but it also brings problems, such as crime, bullying and data leaks, which can affect users everywhere.

Deutschland / Germany

92 haben einen Internetzugang / have Internet access

8 haben keinen Internetzugang / have no Internet access

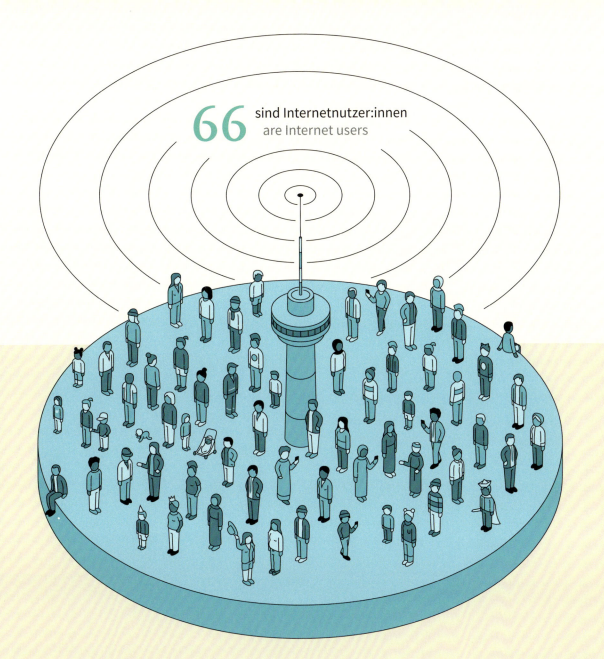
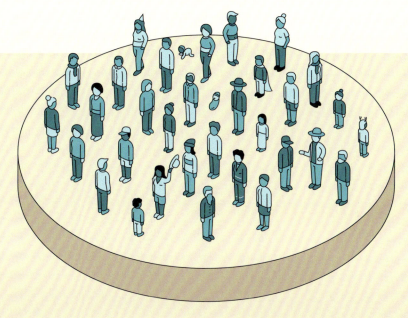

66 sind Internetnutzer:innen
are Internet users

34 sind keine Internetnutzer:innen
are not Internet users

26 Reisen ins Ausland
Travel abroad

Im Sommerurlaub nach Dänemark, Spanien oder Italien? Für viele von uns sind Reisen ins Ausland etwas Schönes, das zum Leben dazugehört. Für die meisten Menschen weltweit ist es aber gar nicht möglich, die Grenzen ihres Landes zu überqueren. Oft fehlt ihnen das Geld für eine Reise in ein anderes Land. 2024 reisten von den 100 Einwohner:innen unseres globalen Dorfes nur 17 Personen ins Ausland. Der Tourismus trägt in viele Ländern zu einem bedeutenden Teil der Wirtschaftsleistung bei: Hotels, Restaurants oder Geschäfte haben Tourist:innen als Kundschaft und können durch sie Geld verdienen und Arbeitsplätze schaffen. Die Zahl der international Reisenden wächst weiterhin. Der Nahe Osten legt dabei prozentual am stärksten zu, gefolgt von Europa, Afrika und der Region Asien-Pazifik.

A summer vacation in Denmark, Spain or Italy? For many of us, traveling abroad is a very appealing part of life. Most people around the world, however, are not able to cross national borders. Often, they do not have the money to visit another country. In 2024, only 17 of our global village's 100 residents traveled abroad. Tourism is an important economic factor in many countries, since tourists frequent hotels, restaurants and shops as customers, allowing locals to earn money and create jobs. The number of international travelers continues to grow. The Middle East is exhibiting the greatest percentual growth, followed by Europe, Africa and the Asia-Pacific region.

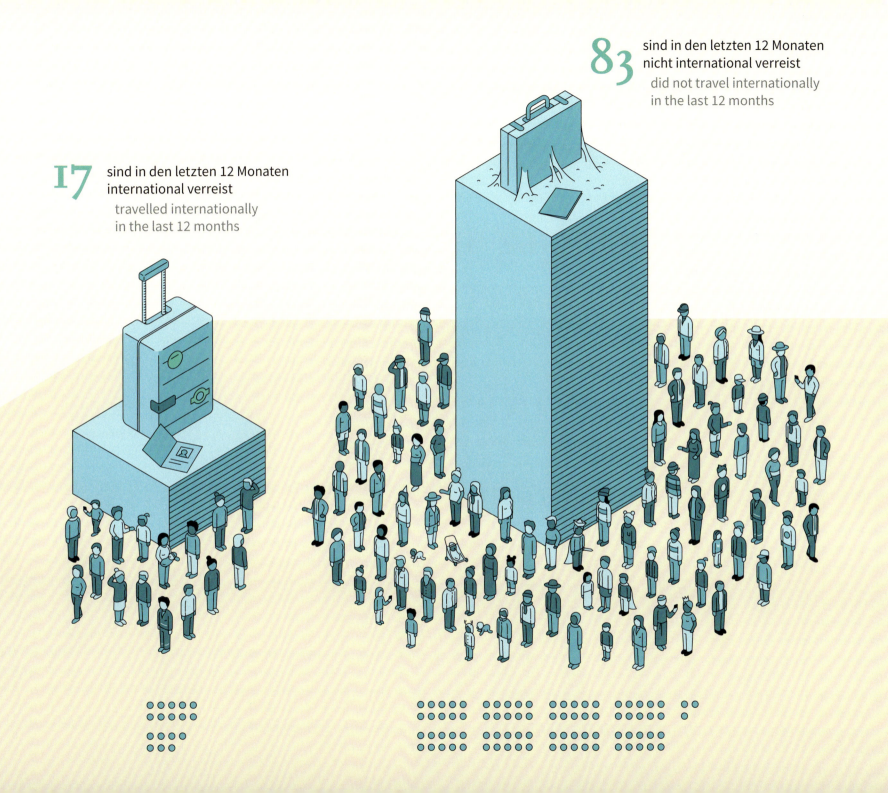

27 Smartphones
Smartphones

Das Smartphone hat sehr viele unserer Lebensbereiche verändert. Heutzutage vereint das Gerät Funktionen, die uns Menschen den Alltag vereinfachen und für die man früher mehrere Technikprodukte benötigte: Wecker, Foto- und Videokamera, Festnetztelefon, Navigationsgerät, Taschenlampe, Radio, Armbanduhr, Ticketautomat für Bus und Bahn, Babyphone … Doch jede technische Revolution hat auch ihre Schattenseiten. Das Smartphone kann süchtig machen und zu Konzentrationsproblemen und Einsamkeit führen. Für die Produktion werden außerdem oft große Mengen an seltenen Metallen und viel Energie benötigt. Teile dieser Ressourcen stammen meistens aus Ländern im Globalen Süden mit unzureichenden Schutzmaßnahmen für Mensch und Natur.

The smartphone has changed many areas of our lives. It fulfills several roles, simplifying daily tasks and replacing a number of other gadgets: alarm clocks, cameras, landline phones, navigation devices, flashlights, radios, wristwatches, ticket machines, baby monitors, etc. Yet every technical revolution also has its downsides. Smartphones can be addictive and can result in people having difficulty concentrating or in their experiencing feelings of loneliness. Moreover, manufacturing them often requires large amounts of rare metals and a lot of energy. Some of these resources come primarily from countries in the Global South, where they are extracted without adequate protection for people or nature.

Deutschland / Germany

80 sind Smartphonenutzer:innen / are not smartphone users

20 sind keine Smartphonenutzer:innen / are not smartphone users

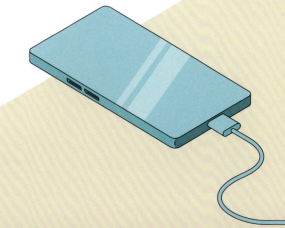

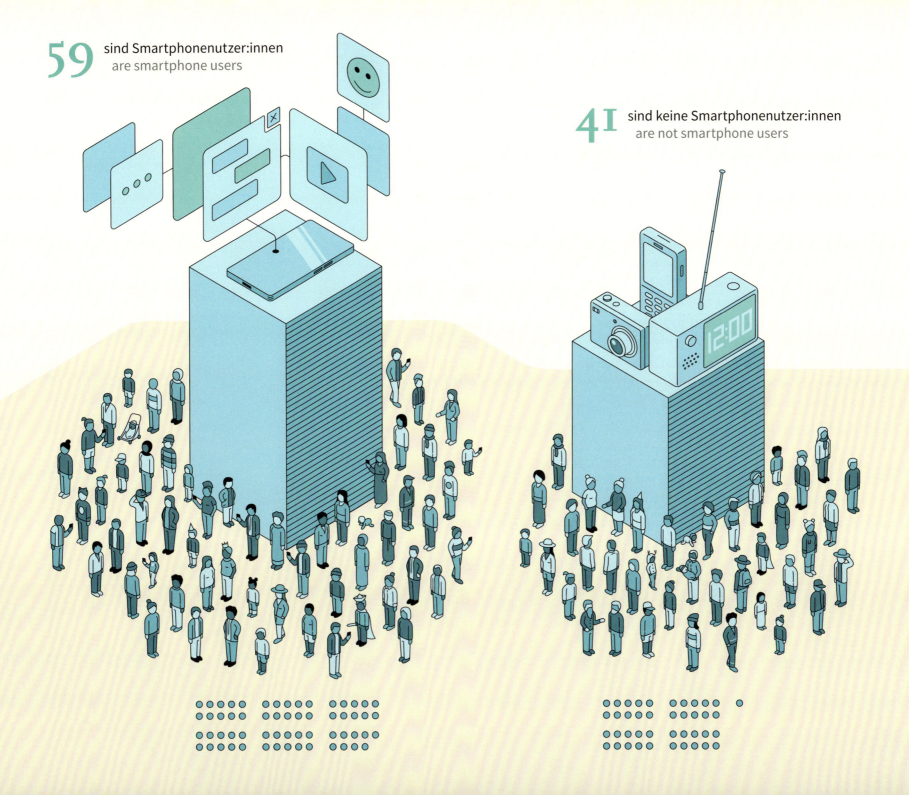

28 Autos
Cars

In vielen Ländern gehört das Auto immer noch zu den gefragtesten Fortbewegungsmitteln. Rund 1,6 Milliarden Autos wurden 2020 auf der ganzen Welt gefahren; viele davon werden privat genutzt. Oft ist ein eigener Pkw (Personenkraftwagen) die einzige Möglichkeit, sich von einem Ort zu einem anderen zu bewegen. Das trifft auch in Deutschland auf viele ländliche Regionen zu. In etlichen Ländern gilt ein eigenes Auto noch immer als Statussymbol: Dem Besitzer geht es beim Kauf nicht nur darum, den Pkw als Transportmittel zu nutzen, sondern mit der Marke und dem Modell zu zeigen, dass er sich ein besonderes Auto leisten kann. Hierzulande und in anderen europäischen Ländern ist jungen Leuten zumindest in Städten mit gut ausgebautem öffentlichem Nahverkehr ein eigenes Fahrzeug nicht mehr so wichtig wie früher. Es gibt dort oftmals Alternativen zum eigenen Auto: Carsharing, E-Roller, E-Bike, Lastenfahrrad oder Fahrgemeinschaft.

In many countries, the car is still one of the most popular means of transport. Around 1.6 billion cars were being driven around the world in 2020, many of them for private use. Often, having your own car is the only way to get from A to B. This is also the case in many rural regions in Germany. In many countries, owning a car is still seen as a status symbol: When people buy one, they do so not only to get around, but also to show they can afford a particular brand or model. For young people in Germany and other European countries, having their own vehicle is no longer as important as it used to be, at least in cities with well-developed public transport networks. There are also alternatives to owning a car, such as car sharing, e-scooters, e-bikes, cargo bikes and carpooling.

Deutschland / Germany

77 haben mindestens ein Auto im Haushalt
have at least one car in their household

23 haben kein Auto im Haushalt
have no car in their household

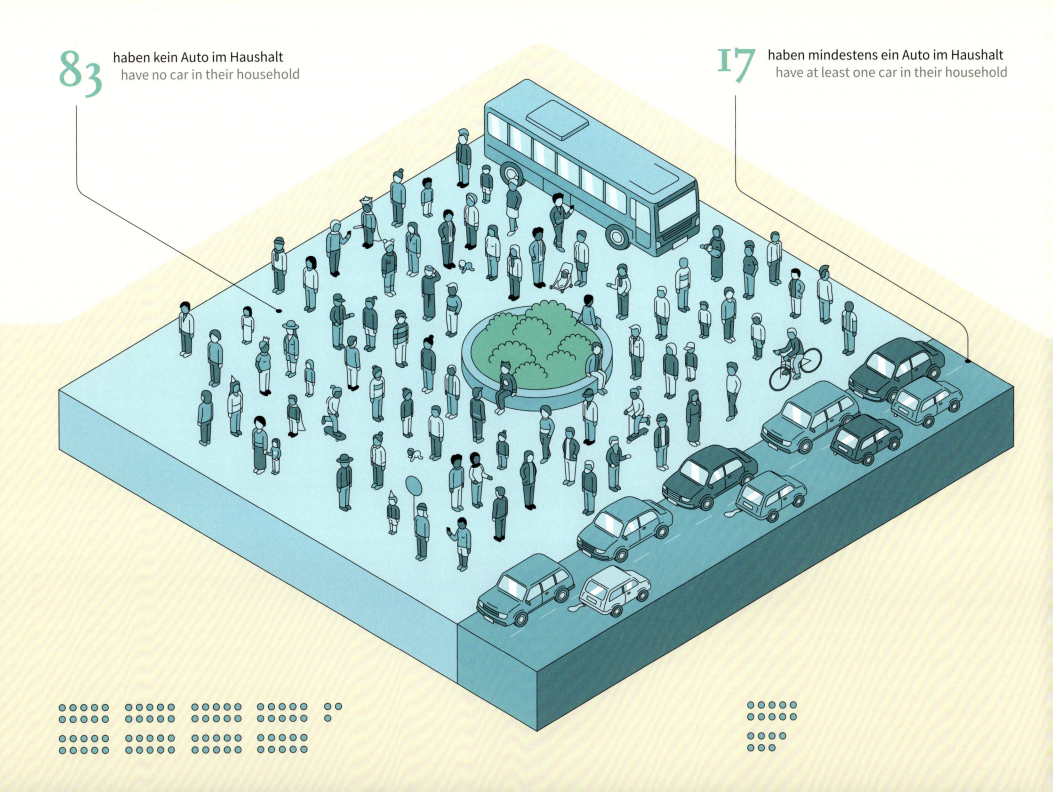

29 CO$_2$-Emissionen
CO$_2$ emissions

Kohlen(stoff)dioxid wird CO$_2$ abgekürzt: ein Gas, das Teil unserer Luft ist. Man kann es weder sehen noch riechen oder schmecken, aber trotzdem ist es wichtig für uns. Wenn wir Luft mit Sauerstoff einatmen, atmen wir Kohlendioxid aus. Pflanzen nehmen das Gas auf und wandeln es wieder in Sauerstoff um. CO$_2$ wird aber auch ausgestoßen, wenn wir Benzin im Automotor verbrennen, oder beim Heizen mit Öl oder Gas. Zu viel CO$_2$ in der Luft lässt die Temperaturen weltweit steigen. In der Folge wandelt sich das Klima und das kann negative Folgen für uns Menschen und die Natur haben. Daher ist es sinnvoll, den Ausstoß von Kohlendioxid zu verringern. Aber nicht alle Personen produzieren gleich viel CO$_2$. Wer oft Auto fährt, mit dem Flugzeug fliegt, Fleisch isst, sehr oft neue Kleidung und andere Produkte kauft, erzeugt mit seinem Handeln mehr Kohlendioxid als jemand, der sich vegetarisch ernährt, alle Wege mit dem Rad zurücklegt und wenig konsumiert. Das sehen wir auch in unserem globalen Dorf: Nur zehn Bewohner:innen sind für knapp die Hälfte aller Kohlendioxid-Emissionen verantwortlich.

Carbon dioxide is abbreviated CO$_2$ and is a gas present in the air we breathe. You can't see, smell or taste it, but it's still important. We inhale air because we need oxygen, but we breathe out carbon dioxide. Plants absorb it and convert it back into oxygen. Yet CO$_2$ is also produced when cars burn gasoline or when we heat our homes with oil or gas. Too much CO$_2$ in the air is causing temperatures to rise worldwide. This is called climate change and can have negative consequences for both humans and nature, which is why it makes sense to reduce emissions of CO$_2$. But not everyone produces the same amount. Anyone who drives a car, flies in a plane or eats meat, or frequently buys new clothes and other products produces more CO$_2$ than someone who eats a vegetarian diet, goes everywhere by bike and consumes less. We can also see this in our global village, where only 10 people are responsible for almost half of all CO$_2$ emissions.

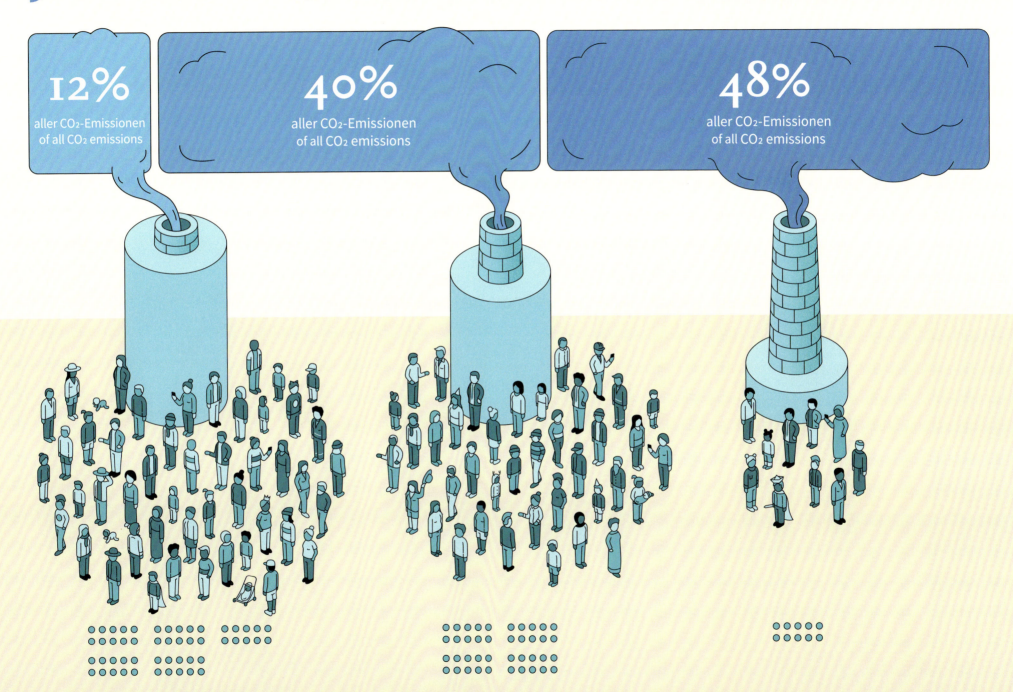

30 Bedrohungen durch den Klimawandel
Threats from climate change

Wetterveränderungen, Fluten und Dürren haben nicht nur Auswirkungen auf die Natur und die Tierwelt. Durch das Erwärmen der Ozeane und die Veränderung des Klimas ist auch der Mensch betroffen. Bereits heute werden Menschen direkt an ihren Wohnorten bedroht, wenn diese besonders nah an Gewässern oder in Risikogebieten liegen. Höhere Temperaturen weltweit bringen das Eis in den Polarregionen zum Schmelzen, wodurch der Meeresspiegel steigt. Küstenorte in aller Welt sind durch den immer höheren Wasserstand der Ozeane direkt von Überschwemmungen bedroht. Jährlich neue Hitzerekorde sorgen dafür, dass Ernten schlechter werden oder ganz ausbleiben. Das gefährdet die Versorgung der Bevölkerung mit Lebensmitteln. Hiervon sind vor allem Menschen im Globalen Süden betroffen, weil sie sich oft mit selbst angebauten Nahrungsmitteln versorgen. Fast jeder zweite Mensch leidet unter den Folgen des Klimawandels.

Floods, droughts and other extreme weather events have an impact on more than just nature and wildlife. As the oceans get warmer and the climate changes, humans are also affected. On the one hand, people are already threatened if they live close to the water or in other at-risk areas. Higher temperatures worldwide are melting polar ice, causing sea levels to rise. Coastal communities around the world are at direct risk of flooding due to surging oceans. Every year, record heat is causing harvests to decline or fail completely, endangering the world's food supply. People in the Global South are particularly affected here, since they often rely on home-grown crops. Almost every second person is impacted by the consequences of climate change.

31 Leben in Konfliktregionen
Life in conflict regions

Viele Menschen leben in Ländern und Regionen, die nicht sicher sind. Konflikte, Krisen, Kriege und Instabilität machen den Alltag dort schwierig. In den vergangenen Jahren ist die Zahl der Betroffenen gestiegen: Weltweit lebt jede vierte Person an diesen Orten – das sind zwei der acht Milliarden Menschen. Einige Kriege und Krisen sehen wir in den Nachrichten, aber viele erhalten kaum Aufmerksamkeit. Die Menschen dort müssen trotzdem unter schwierigen Lebensbedingungen ihren Alltag bestreiten. Das Heidelberger Institut für Internationale Konfliktforschung (HIIK) zählte 2023 mehr als 350 Konflikte, die meisten davon im Raum Asien und Ozeanien. Internationale Organisationen wie die Vereinten Nationen arbeiten daran, den Einwohner:innen dieser Gebiete zu helfen und dauerhafte Lösungen der Konflikte zu erreichen.

Many people live in countries and regions that are not safe, areas where conflicts, crises, wars or instability make everyday life difficult. The number of those residing in such areas has increased in recent years: One in four people worldwide now lives in an unsafe place – two billion of the world's eight billion people. Some crises and wars appear in the news, but many receive little media attention – yet people in those areas still have to go about their everyday lives despite the difficult conditions. The Heidelberg Institute for International Conflict Research has identified more than 350 conflicts worldwide in 2023, most of them in Asia and Oceania. International organizations such as the United Nations are working to help people living in these areas by finding lasting solutions to the conflicts.

32 Demokratien und Autokratien
Democracies and autocracies

Alle Länder der Welt lassen sich in zwei politische Kategorien einteilen: Demokratien und Autokratien. Demokratisch sind die Staaten, in denen es freie Wahlen gibt und die Menschen so über ihre Regierungen entscheiden und sie auch abwählen können. Außerdem gibt es eine Gewaltenteilung. Das bedeutet, dass die Macht im Staat auf verschiedene Organe aufgeteilt ist: Es gibt die gesetzgebende Gewalt (Legislative), die ausführende Gewalt (Exekutive) und die rechtsprechende Gewalt (Judikative). In Autokratien gibt es weder freie Wahlen noch eine funktionierende Gewaltenteilung. Dort liegt die Macht in den Händen einer Person oder einer kleinen Gruppe von Menschen und das Volk hat wenig oder gar keine Möglichkeiten, dies zu ändern. In unserem globalen Dorf leben mehr als zwei Drittel der Menschen in autokratischen Systemen und weniger als ein Drittel in Demokratien.

All of the world's countries can be divided politically into two categories: democracies and autocracies. Democratic states are those in which there are free elections, meaning people can choose their government and vote it out of office. There is also a separation of powers, which means that power is divided between different government organs: the legislative, executive and judiciary. Autocracies have neither free elections nor a functioning separation of powers. There, power lies in the hands of one person or a small group, a situation ordinary citizens have little or no ability to change. More than two-thirds of the people residing in our global village live in autocracies and less than one-third in democracies.

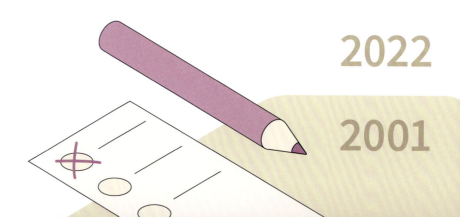

2022

2001

28 leben in Demokratien
live in democracies

72 leben in Autokratien
live in autocracies

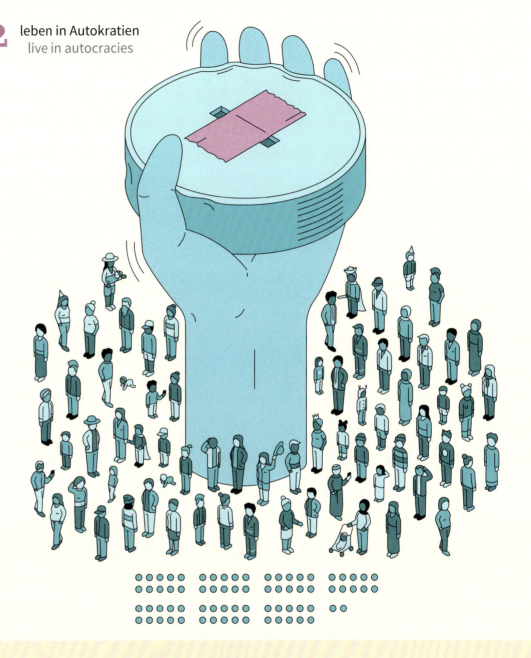

33 Sicherheit
Safety

Der Heimweg von einer Party oder der Weg frühmorgens zur Arbeit – vielen Menschen flößen Wege im Dunkeln auch in der eigenen Nachbarschaft Furcht ein. Weltweit fühlen sich zwar zwei Drittel der Bevölkerung sicher, aber ein Drittel hat Angst. Regional besonders hoch ist diese Zahl in Lateinamerika und der Karibik. In Europa, Nordamerika sowie Zentral- und Südasien fühlen sich die Menschen sicherer. Oft sind es – unabhängig von der Region – Frauen, die sich nachts unsicher fühlen. Das kann langfristig zu Stress und zu Angstzuständen führen. Die Sicherheit der Bevölkerung hat also nicht nur direkte, sondern auch indirekte Folgen für das persönliche Wohlbefinden.

Strolling home from a party or going to work before sunrise – for many people, walking in the dark, even in their own neighborhood, is frightening. Although two-thirds of the world's inhabitants feel safe, one-third are afraid. The figure is particularly high in Latin America and the Caribbean. People feel safer in Europe, North America and Central and South Asia. Regardless of the region, it is often women who feel unsafe at night, something that can lead to stress and anxiety over the long term. Safety can therefore have a direct and indirect impact on individual well-being.

67 fühlen sich nachts in ihrer Nachbarschaft sicher
feel safe walking in their neighborhood at night

33 haben ein Gefühl von Unsicherheit nachts in ihrer Nachbarschaft
do not feel safe walking in their neighborhood at night

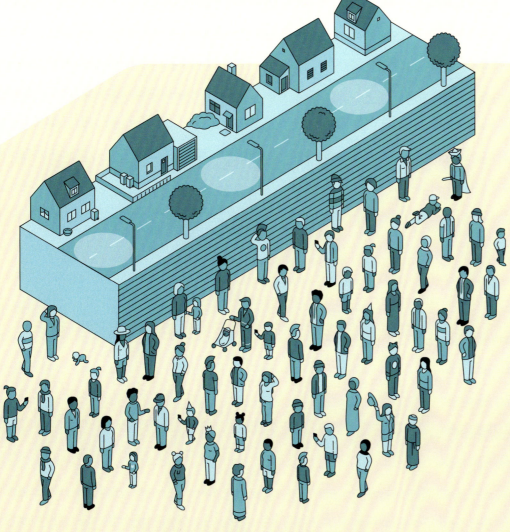

34 Bürgerliche Freiheiten
Civil liberties

Freiheit zu definieren, ist nicht einfach. Auch, weil Freiheitsbegriffe einem ständigen Wandel unterliegen. Was vor einigen Jahren noch als frei betrachtet wurde, gilt heute nicht mehr unbedingt. Die internationale Nichtregierungsorganisation Freedom House hat ein Kategoriensystem erstellt, das trotzdem versucht, Freiheit zu definieren. Dabei werden individuelle Freiheiten wie ein allgemeines Wahlrecht, die persönliche Entwicklung oder die Gleichheit vor dem Gesetz berücksichtigt. Daraus entsteht der Gobal Freedom Score, der alle Menschen je nach den Bedingungen in ihren Ländern in drei Kategorien einteilt: frei, teilweise frei und nicht frei. Die größte Gruppe der Dorfbewohner:innen ist laut diesem Index in ihren bürgerlichen Rechten nicht frei.

Defining freedom is not easy. After all, the concept of freedom is subject to constant change. What was considered "free" a few years ago is no longer necessarily viewed the same way today. The international non-governmental organization Freedom House has created a classification system that attempts to define freedom nevertheless. The systems takes into account individual freedoms, such as universal suffrage, personal development and equality before the law. The result is the Global Freedom Score, which divides all people into three categories – free, partly free and not free – depending on the conditions found in the country where they live. According to this index, in terms of civil rights, the largest group of villagers is not free.

21 sind frei
are free

41 sind teilweise frei
are partly free

38 sind nicht frei
are not free

35 Zugang zum Rechtsstaat
Access to rule of law

Gesetze gelten in der Theorie für alle Bürger:innen eines Landes. Wenn jemand eine Person in ihren Rechten verletzt, zum Beispiel ihr etwas stiehlt, sie verletzt oder beleidigt, kann diese den Täter bzw. die Täterin – oder sogar den Staat, wenn dieser Unrecht anwendet – verklagen und sollten dann auch Recht bekommen. Das gilt zumindest in der Theorie. In der Praxis haben viele Menschen aber keinen Zugang zum Rechtsstaat. Das bedeutet, sie können ihre Rechte nicht geltend machen. In vielen Ländern haben diejenigen mit Geld und Macht das Recht auf ihrer Seite. Der Großteil der Bevölkerung hingegen hat keine Möglichkeit, gegen die privilegierte Schicht vorzugehen. Das ist zwar ungerecht, aber leider für etwa zwei Drittel der Dorfbewohner:innen Realität.

In theory, laws apply equally to all of a country's citizens. If someone's rights have been violated – if something has been stolen from them, for example, or they have been injured or slandered – they can sue the perpetrator, even the state if it's the one acting improperly, to obtain justice. At least in theory. In practice, however, many people have no access to the rule of law, which means they cannot assert their rights. In many countries, those with money and power have the law on their side. The majority of the population, on the other hand, has no opportunity to take action against the privileged class. Although this is unfair, it's the reality faced by some two-thirds of the people in our global village.

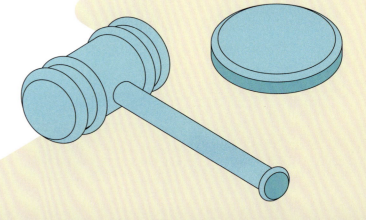

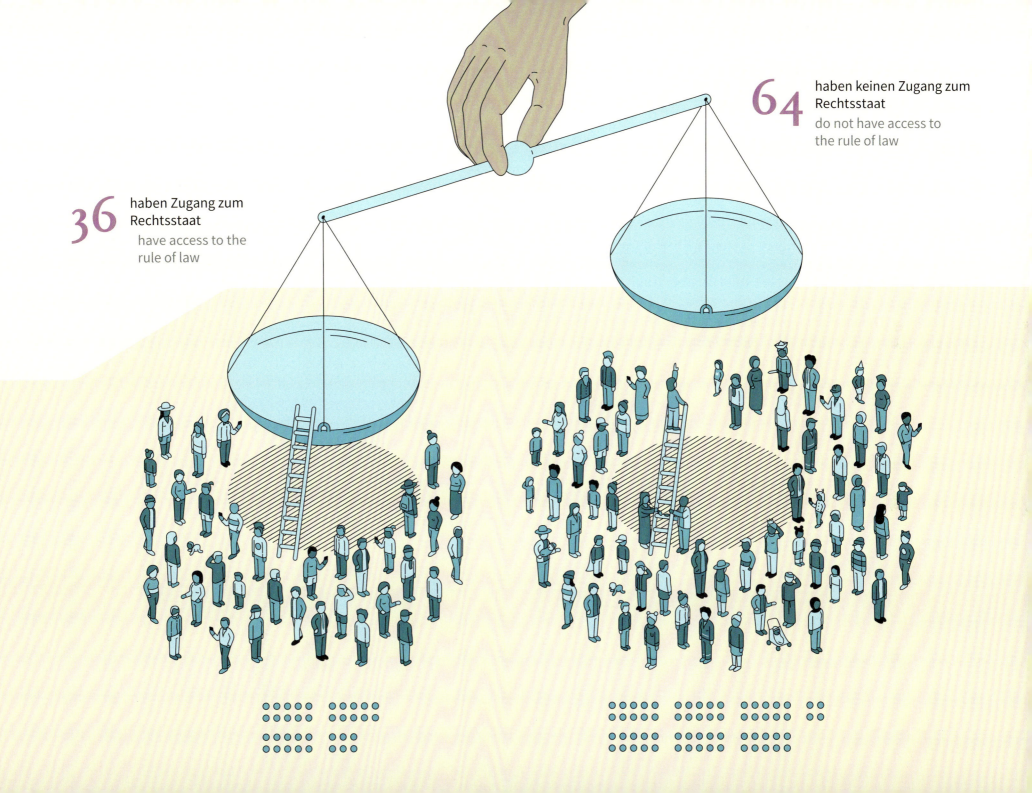

36 Akademische Freiheit
Academic freedom

Universitäten und Forschungseinrichtungen können nur dann uneingeschränkt arbeiten, wenn für sie die akademische Freiheit gilt. Das bedeutet, dass sie ihre Forschung und Lehre nach wissenschaftlichen Kriterien gestalten können, ohne dass der Staat oder andere Institutionen sie dabei beeinflussen. Das Konzept der Wissenschaftsfreiheit ist sehr alt und geht auf den Philosophen Platon zurück, der sie vor mehr als 2.400 Jahren im antiken Griechenland formuliert hat. In vielen Ländern, darunter auch Deutschland, ist sie in der Verfassung verankert. Der Academic Freedom Index bewertet die weltweite Entwicklung. Aktuell geht die akademische Freiheit für unsere Dorfbewohner:innen zurück – vor allem in bevölkerungsreichen Ländern.

Universities and research institutions can only work without interference if they enjoy academic freedom. This means being able to conduct their research and teaching according to scientific criteria without being influenced by the state or other institutions. The idea of academic freedom is very old; it goes back to the philosopher Plato, who advanced the concept more than 2,400 years ago in ancient Greece. In many countries, including Germany, it's anchored in the constitution. The Academic Freedom Index tracks the state of teaching and research worldwide. Currently, our villagers are experiencing declining levels of academic freedom – especially in more populous countries.

50 haben akademische Freiheit
have academic freedom

50 haben keine akademische Freiheit
do not have academic freedom

37 Pressefreiheit
Freedom of the press

Freie und unabhängige Medien – also Zeitungen und Zeitschriften, Radio und Fernsehen, Internet und soziale Medien – sind wichtige Bestandteile von Demokratien. Die Journalist:innen informieren die Bevölkerung unabhängig von Staat und Parteien, tragen zur öffentlichen Meinungsbildung bei und benennen gesellschaftliche Probleme und Missstände. Damit sie frei arbeiten können und keine Angst vor negativen Konsequenzen haben müssen, wenn sie zum Beispiel die Regierung kritisieren, gilt für sie die Pressefreiheit. In vielen Ländern funktioniert das aber leider nicht. Dort kann eine unerwünschte Berichterstattung für die Medienschaffenden negative persönliche Folgen haben: von Bedrohungen und Einschränkungen der journalistischen Arbeit bis hin zu Strafverfolgung, Gefängnis oder Tod.

Free and independent media – newspapers and magazines, radio and television, the Internet and social media – are an important part of democracy. Uninfluenced by the state and political parties, journalists provide people with information, helping form public opinion and identifying social problems and injustices. Freedom of the press is needed so journalists can work independently and not fear retaliation – if they criticize the government, for example. Unfortunately, this is not the case in many countries. There, unwanted reporting can have negative personal repercussions for media professionals that range from threats and restrictions on their journalistic activities to criminal prosecution, prison and even death.

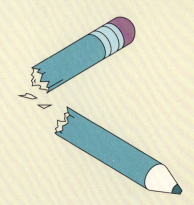

13 gut bis zufriedenstellend
good, satisfactory

13 problematisch
problematic

22 schwierig
difficult

52 sehr ernst
very serious

38 Korruption
Corruption

Wer sich von jemand anderem bestechen lässt oder selbst besticht, ist korrupt, begeht also Korruption. Das ist zum Beispiel der Fall, wenn jemand Vorteile gegen Geld in Anspruch nimmt, obwohl das illegal ist. So ein Fall liegt vor, wenn ein Unternehmen eine:n Politiker:in bezahlt, damit die Firma bei der Vergabe öffentlicher Aufträge bevorzugt wird. Oder wenn man einem Antrag auf dem Bürgeramt ein Geschenk beifügt, damit das Anliegen schneller bearbeitet wird. Die Nichtregierungsorganisation Transparency International untersucht, wie viel Korruption Menschen in ihrem Land wahrnehmen. Daraus wird eine Skala erstellt: Je niedriger der Wert, desto eher herrschen korrupte Praktiken im Land. 60 der 100 Dorfbewohner:innen leben in Staaten mit weit verbreiteter Korruption.

Anyone who accepts a bribe or bribes someone else is engaging in corruption. This is the case when someone pays for certain advantages even though it's illegal. For example, if a company gives a politician money to ensure it receives preferential treatment when a public contract is awarded. Or if someone includes a gift when submitting an application to local authorities so that the application is processed more quickly. The non-governmental organization Transparency International studies how people perceive the level of corruption in their country. It rates their perceptions on a scale: The lower the number, the more likely it is that corrupt practices are taking place. In our global village, 60 of the 100 inhabitants live in countries with widespread corruption.

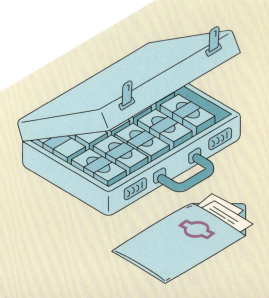

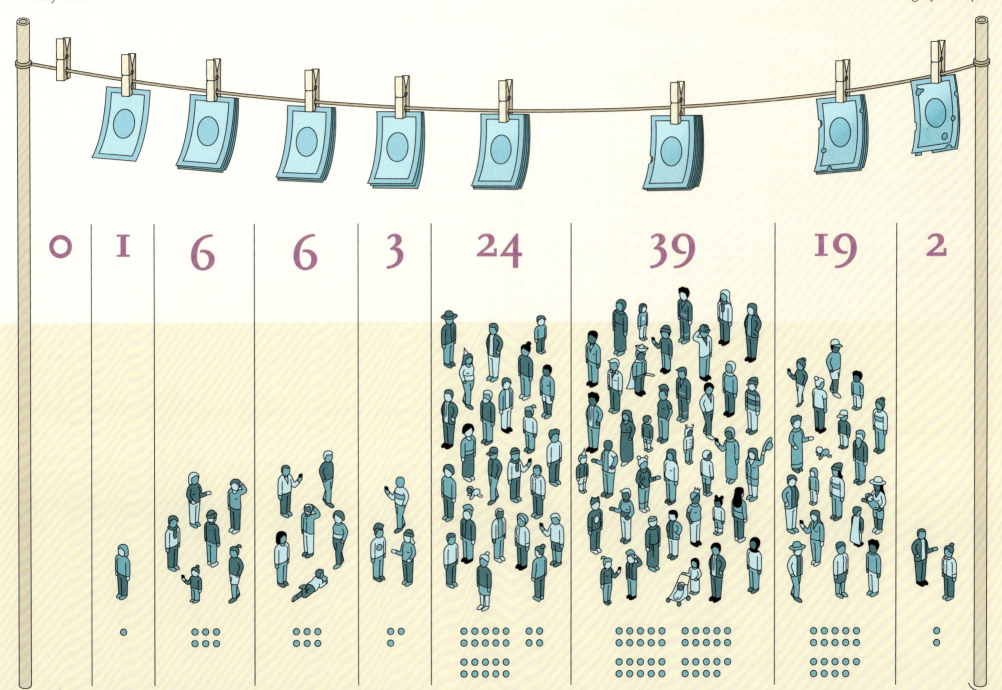

39 Geschlechtergerechtigkeit
Gender equality

Die gleichen Rechte und Chancen im Leben zu haben, unabhängig vom Geschlecht, das ist leider für viele Frauen und Mädchen weltweit nur ein Traum. Der Gender Equality Index misst anhand von rechtlichen und gesellschaftlichen Rahmenstrukturen die Gleichstellung der Geschlechter. Dabei wird unter anderem betrachtet, ob Frauen und Mädchen gleichberechtigt sind in Kategorien wie der Personenfreizügigkeit, dem Arbeitsrecht, der Entlohnung, dem Ehe- und Eigentumsrecht. Das heißt: Dürfen sie – so wie Männer und Jungen – selbst bestimmen, wo sie leben und was sie arbeiten? Werden sie für dieselben Jobs genauso bezahlt? Dürfen sie entscheiden, wen sie heiraten, und ohne Erlaubnis von Vater, Bruder oder Ehemann kaufen, was sie möchten?

Unfortunately, for many women and girls around the world, having the same rights and opportunities in life despite their gender is still just a dream. The Gender Equality Index measures gender equality based on legal and social conditions. Among other things, it considers whether women and girls are equal in terms of freedom of movement, employment and remuneration, as well as marriage laws and property rights. That means, can they, like men and boys, decide for themselves where they live and what their occupation is? Do they receive equal pay for equal work? Can they decide whom they marry? And can they buy what they want without getting permission from their father, brother or husband?

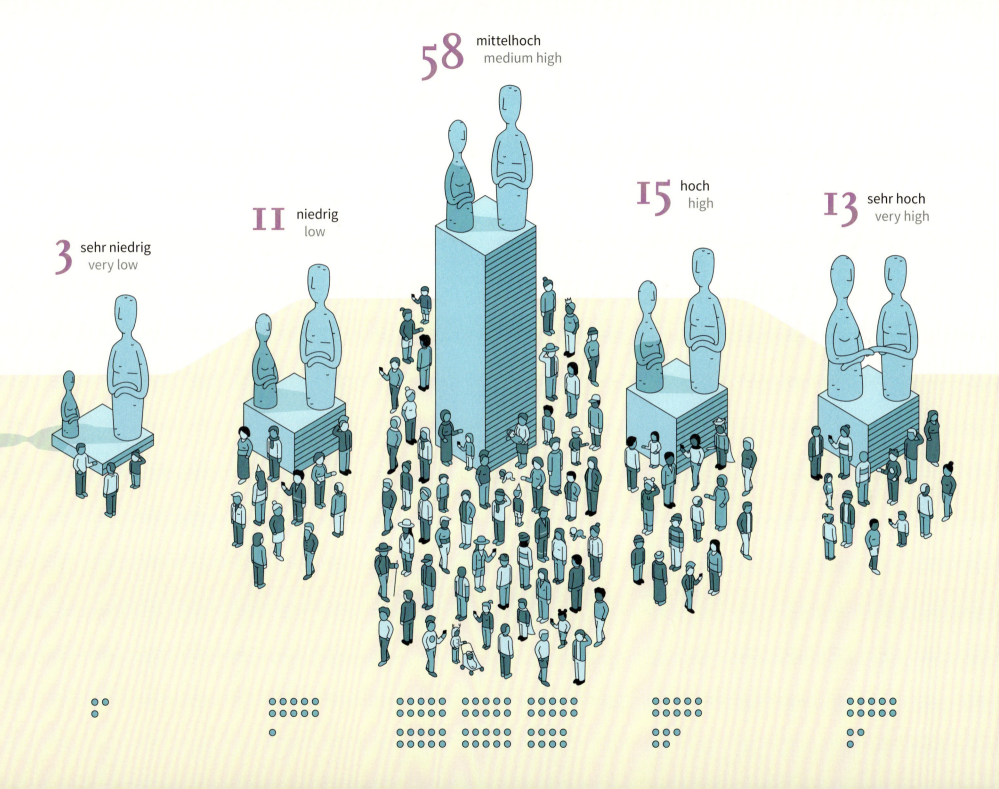

40 Gleichgeschlechtliche Ehe
Same-sex marriage

Die Niederlande waren 2001 das erste Land weltweit, das gleichgeschlechtlichen Paaren erlaubt hat zu heiraten. In den folgenden Dekaden sind mehrere Dutzend weitere Staaten gefolgt – vor allem in Westeuropa und auf dem amerikanischen Kontinent. In vielen Ländern gab es zunächst die Möglichkeit, eine Lebenspartnerschaft eintragen zu lassen, quasi eine „Ehe light" mit weniger Rechten, bevor die komplette Gleichstellung politisch beschlossen wurde. Das war in Deutschland ebenfalls so. Auch wenn in immer mehr Staaten queere Paare rechtlich gleichgestellt werden mit heterosexuellen Paaren, gibt es immer noch Länder, in denen Menschen, die ihre Homosexualität offen leben, bestraft werden – im schlimmsten Fall sogar mit der Todesstrafe.

In 2001, the Netherlands became the first country in the world to allow same-sex couples to marry. In subsequent decades, several dozen other countries followed – especially in Western Europe and North and South America. Many countries initially allowed people to enter into a civil partnership, a kind of "marriage light" with fewer rights, before eventually offering complete equality – something that was also the case in Germany. Even though more and more countries now treat queer and heterosexual couples equally before the law, there are still states in which homosexuals are punished for expressing their sexuality – in the worst case, even with the death penalty.

17 rechtliche Gleichstellung der gleichgeschlechtlichen Ehe
equal rights for same-sex marriage

59 keine Strafverfolgung, keine gleichgeschlechtliche Ehe
no prosecution, no same sex-marriage

24 Homosexualität illegal
homosexuality illegal

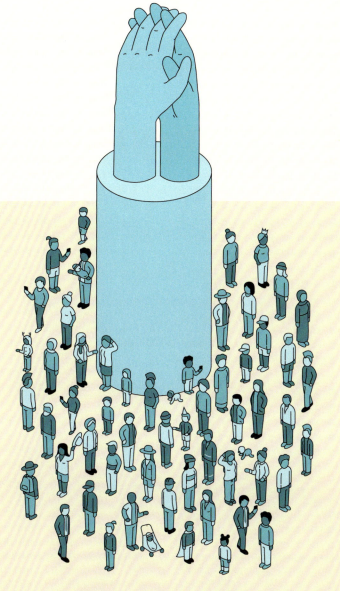

Quellenverzeichnis
Source list

Ein ausführliches und kommentiertes Literaturverzeichnis zu diesem Buch finden Sie online unter den folgenden QR-Codes. Scannen Sie einfach die QR-Codes mit Ihrem Smartphone oder Tablet, um direkt zu den entsprechenden Inhalten zu gelangen.

A detailed and annotated bibliography for this book is available online via the following QR codes. Simply scan the QR codes with your smartphone or tablet to access the content directly.

bertelsmann-stiftung.de/100menschen/

bertelsmann-stiftung.de/100people/

1 Kontinent / Continents
Deutsche Stiftung Weltbevölkerung (DSW) (2022). *DSW-Datenreport 2022. Soziale und demografische Daten weltweit.* Hannover. S. 8 ff. https://www.dsw.org/wp-content/uploads/2023/11/DSW-Datenreport_2022_web.pdf. Download 4.3.2025.

Deutsche Stiftung Weltbevölkerung (2025). Weltbevölkerung. https://www.dsw.org/weltbevoelkerung/. Download 16.3.2025.

2 Länder / Countries
Deutsche Stiftung Weltbevölkerung (DSW) (2022). *DSW-Datenreport 2022. Soziale und demografische Daten weltweit.* Hannover. S. 8 ff. https://www.dsw.org/wp-content/uploads/2023/11/DSW-Datenreport_2022_web.pdf. Download 4.3.2025.

United Nations Department of Economic and Social Affairs, Sara Hertog, Patrick Gerland und John Wilmoth (2023). *India Overtakes China as the World's Most Populous Country.* UN Department of Economic and Social Affairs (DESA) Policy Briefs. 15.6.2023. DOI: https://doi.org/10.18356/27081990-153. Download 16.3.2025.

3 Alter / Age
Deutsche Stiftung Weltbevölkerung (DSW) (2022). *DSW-Datenreport 2022. Soziale und demografische Daten weltweit.* Hannover. S. 3. https://www.dsw.org/wp-content/uploads/2023/11/DSW-Datenreport_2022_web.pdf. Download 4.3.2025.

4 Muttersprachen / Native languages
CIA (2023). The World Fact Book. https://www.cia.gov/the-world-factbook/about/archives/2023/countries/world/. Download 4.3.2025.

Zimmermann, Klaus (2016). „7. Missionarslinguistik in kolonialen Kontexten. Ein historischer Überblick". *Sprache und Kolonialismus: Eine interdisziplinäre Einführung zu Sprache und Kommunikation in kolonialen Kontexten* (Hrsg.) Thomas Stolz, Ingo H. Warnke und Daniel Schmidt-Brücken. Berlin und Boston. S. 169–192. https://doi.org/10.1515/9783110370904-008. Download 16.3.2025.

5 Weltsprachen / World languages
CIA (2023). *The World Fact Book.* https://www.cia.gov/the-world-factbook/about/archives/2023/countries/world/. Download 4.3.2025.

Zimmermann, Klaus (2016). „7. Missionarslinguistik in kolonialen Kontexten. Ein historischer Überblick". *Sprache und Kolonialismus: Eine interdisziplinäre Einführung zu Sprache und Kommunikation in kolonialen Kontexten* (Hrsg.) Thomas Stolz, Ingo H. Warnke und Daniel Schmidt-Brücken. Berlin und Boston. S. 169–192. https://doi.org/10.1515/9783110370904-008. Download 16.3.2025.

6 Religion / Religion
Forschungsgruppe Weltanschauungen in Deutschland (fowid) (2024). *Religionszugehörigkeiten 2023.* https://fowid.de/meldung/religionszugehoerigkeiten-2023. Download 16.3.2025.

Pew Research Center (2022). *Religious Composition by Country, 2010–2050.* https://www.pewresearch.org/religion/feature/religious-composition-by-country-2010-2050/. Download 4.3.2025.

7 Wohnort / Place of residence
World Bank Group (2023). *Urban Development.* https://www.worldbank.org/en/topic/urbandevelopment/overview. Download 4.3.2025.

World Bank Group (2025). *Urban population* (% of total population). https://data.worldbank.org/indicator/SP.URB.TOTL.IN.ZS. Download 4.3.2025.

8 Armenviertel / Slums
United Nations (2023). *The Sustainable Development Goals Report 2023: Special edition. Towards a Rescue Plan for People and Planet.* New York. https://unstats.un.org/sdgs/report/2023/The-Sustainable-Development-Goals-Report-2023.pdf. Download 4.3.2025.

United Nations Statistics Division (2025). *SDG indicators. Goal 11.* https://unstats.un.org/sdgs/report/2024/Goal-11/#:~:text=Globally%2C%20approximately%20one%20quarter%20of,10%20individuals%20have%20convenient%20access. Download 16.3.2025.

9 Analphabetismus / Illiteracy
Bundesministerium für Bildung und Forschung (2025). *Zahlen und Fakten.* https://www.xn--mein-schlssel-zur-welt-0lc.de/de/helfen/zahlen-und-fakten/zahlen-und-fakten.html. Download 4.3.2025.

Statistisches Bundesamt (2025). *Internationales: Alphabetisierung der Weltbevölkerung.* https://www.destatis.de/DE/Themen/Laender-Regionen/Internationales/Thema/bevoelkerung-arbeit-soziales/bildung/Alphabetisierung.html. Download 4.3.2025.

UNESCO (2024). *International Literacy Day, 8 September.* https://www.unesco.org/en/days/literacy. Download 16.3.2025.

10 Bildung / Education
Encyclopedia Britannica (2025). *Education.* https://www.britannica.com/topic/education. Download 16.3.2025.

Statista (2025). *Educational attainment worldwide in 2020, by gender and level.* https://www.statista.com/statistics/1212278/education-gender-gap-worldwide-by-level/. Download 4.3.2025.

11 Arbeit / Work
International Labour Organization (ILO) (2023). *World Employment and Social Outlook. Trends 2023.* Genf. https://www.ilo.org/sites/default/files/wcmsp5/groups/public/%40dgreports/%40inst/documents/publication/wcms_865332.pdf. Download 5.3.2025.

Statistisches Bundesamt (2025). *Konjunkturindikatoren: Erwerbstätige im Inland nach Wirtschaftssektoren.* https://www.destatis.de/DE/Themen/Wirtschaft/Konjunkturindikatoren/Lange-Reihen/Arbeitsmarkt/lrerw13a.html. Download 4.3.2025.

World Bank Group (2025). *Employment in agriculture, industry, and services (% of total employment) (modeled ILO estimate).* https://data.worldbank.org/indicator/SL.AGR.EMPL.ZS. Download 4.3.2025.

World Bank Group (2025). *Employment in services (% of total employment) (modeled ILO estimate).* https://data.worldbank.org/indicator/SL.SRV.EMPL.ZS. Download 4.3.2025.

World Bank Group (2025). *Employment in industry (% of total employment) (modeled ILO estimate).* https://data.worldbank.org/indicator/SL.IND.EMPL.ZS. Download 4.3.2025.

World Bank Group (2025). *Population, total - Germany (2023).* https://data.worldbank.org/indicator/SP.POP.TOTL?locations=DE. Download 4.3.2025.

12 Einkommen / Income
World Bank Group (2024). *The Middle-Income Trap. World Development Report 2024.* Washington D.C. https://www.worldbank.org/en/publication/wdr2024?cid=ECR_E_NewsletterWeekly_EN_EXT&deliveryName=DM226534. Download 4.3.2025.

13 Vermögen / Assets
Shorrocks, Anthony, James Davies und Rodrigo Lluberas (2022). *Global Wealth Databook 2022. Leading perspectives to navigate the future.* Crédit Suisse Research Institute: o.O., S. 21. https://bibbase.org/network/publication/shorrocks-davies-lluberas-globalwealthdatabook2022-2022. Download 4.3.2025.

14 Bankkonto / Bank account
Demirgüç-Kunt, Asli, Leora Klapper, Dorothe Singer und Saniya Ansar (2022). *The Global Findex Database 2021. Financial Inclusion, Digital Payments, and Resilience in the Age of COVID-19.* World Bank Group, Washington D.C. S. 17. https://www.worldbank.org/en/publication/globalfindex/Report. Download 4.3.2025.

15 Krankenversicherung / Health insurance
World Health Organization (WHO) (2023). *Universal health coverage (UHC).* https://www.who.int/news-room/fact-sheets/detail/universal-health-coverage-(uhc). Download 4.3.2025.

16 Psychische Gesundheit / Mental health
World Health Organization (WHO) (2022). *Mental disorders.* https://www.who.int/news-room/fact-sheets/detail/mental-disorders. Download 4.3.2025.
Queensland Brain Institute (2024). *Half of world's population will experience a mental health disorder.* Harvard Medical School. https://hms.harvard.edu/news/half-worlds-population-will-experience-mental-health-disorder. Download 20.3.2025.

17 Fleischkonsum / Meat consumption
Friedrichsen, Jana, und Manja Gärtner (2020). „Why Are We Eating so Much Meat?". DIW Roundup: Politik im Fokus 137. DIW Berlin. https://www.diw.de/documents/publikationen/73/diw_01.c.741618.de/diw_roundup_137_en.pdf. Download 4.3.2025.
IfD Allensbach und Statista (2023). *Anzahl der Personen in Deutschland, die sich selbst als Vegetarier einordnen oder als Leute, die weitgehend auf Fleisch verzichten, von 2015 bis 2023 (in Millionen).* https://de.statista.com/statistik/daten/studie/173636/umfrage/lebenseinstellung-anzahl-vegetarier/. Download 4.3.2025.

18 Laktoseintoleranz / Lactose intolerance
MedlinePlus (2023). *Lactose intolerance.* https://medlineplus.gov/genetics/condition/lactose-intolerance/#frequency. Download 4.3.2025.

19 Übergewicht / Overweight
Statistisches Bundesamt (2025). *Europa: Mehr als die Hälfte der Erwachsenen hat Übergewicht.* https://www.destatis.de/Europa/DE/Thema/Bevoelkerung-Arbeit-Soziales/Gesundheit/Uebergewicht.html. Download 4.3.2025.
World Health Organization (WHO) (2021). *Obesity.* https://www.who.int/news-room/facts-in-pictures/detail/6-facts-on-obesity#:~:text=Overweight%20and%20obesity%20are%20linked,income%20and%20middle%2Dincome%20countries. Download 16.3.2025.
World Health Organization (WHO) (2024). *Obesity and overweight, Key Facts.* https://www.who.int/news-room/fact-sheets/detail/obesity-and-overweight#:~:text=Worldwide%20adult%20obesity%20has%20more,16%25%20were%20living%20with%20obesity. Download 4.3.2025.

20 Unterernährung / Malnutrition
Food and Agriculture Organization of the UN (2015). *The State of Food Insecurity in the World. Meeting the 2015 international hunger targets: taking stock of uneven Progress.* Rom. https://openknowledge.fao.org/server/api/core/bitstreams/63863832-4cb5-4e05-9040-4b22d9a92324/content. Download 4.3.2025.
World Health Organization (2024). *Hunger numbers stubbornly high for three consecutive years as global crises deepen: UN Report (2023).* https://www.who.int/news/item/24-07-2024-hunger-numbers-stubbornly-high-for-three-consecutive-years-as-global-crises-deepen--un-report. Download 4.3.2025.

21 Toiletten / Toilets
Statista (2022). *Bevölkerungsanteil mit Zugang zu sicheren Sanitäranlagen nach Weltregionen im Jahr 2022.* https://de.statista.com/statistik/daten/studie/1021970/umfrage/zugang-zu-sicheren-sanitaeranlagen-nach-weltregionen/. Download 4.3.2025.
World Health Organization (WHO) (2024). *Sanitation.* https://www.who.int/news-room/fact-sheets/detail/sanitation. Download 1.4.2025

22 Sauberes Trinkwasser / Clean drinking water
King, Marcus (2024). *Climate Change and the Water Weapon: How Rising Temperatures are Expanding the Footprint of Conflict.* https://commonhome.georgetown.edu/issues/spring-2024/climate-change-and-the-water-weapon-how-rising-temperatures-are-expanding-the-footprint-of-conflict/. Download 16.3.2025.
Michel, David (2024). *What Causes Water Conflict?* https://www.csis.org/analysis/what-causes-water-conflict. Download 16.3.2025.
United Nations (o.D.). *Human Rights to Water and Sanitation.* https://www.unwater.org/water-facts/human-rights-water-and-sanitation#:~:text=Access%20to%20water%20and%20sanitation,safely%20managed%20water%20and%20sanitation. Download 18.3.2025.
World Health Organization (WHO) (2024). *Proportion of population using safely managed drinking-water services (%).* https://data.who.int/indicators/i/5131A52/1548EA3. Download 4.3.2025.

23 Elektrizität / Electricity
International Energy Forum (2022). *Four Ways Energy Access Will Drive the UN's Sustainable Development Goals.* https://www.ief.org/news/four-ways-energy-access-will-drive-the-uns-sustainable-development-goals. Download 16.3.2025.
United Nations Statistics Division (2025). *Affordable and clean energy.* https://unstats.un.org/sdgs/report/2023/Goal-07/#:~:text=The%20global%20electricity%20access%20rate,2021%2C%20mostly%20located%20in%20LDCs. Download 4.3.2025.
United Nations (o.D.). *Universal Access to Electricity.* https://unite.un.org/sites/unite.un.org/files/app-desa-electrification/index.html. Download 16.3.2025.
World Bank Group (2023). *Access to electricity (% of population).* https://data.worldbank.org/indicator/EG.ELC.ACCS.ZS?end=2021&start=2000. Download 4.3.2025.

24 Waschmaschinen / Washing machines
International Energy Agency (IEA) (2023). *Global average household ownership of appliances in the Net Zero Scenario, 2000–2030.* https://www.iea.org/data-and-statistics/charts/global-average-household-ownership-of-appliances-in-the-net-zero-scenario-2000-2030. Download 4.3.2025.
Statista (2021). *Anteil der privaten Haushalte in Deutschland mit einer Waschmaschine von 2011 bis 2021.* https://de.statista.com/statistik/daten/studie/516859/umfrage/private-haushalte-in-deutschland-mit-waschmaschine/. Download 4.3.2025.

25 Internetzugang / Internet access
Heinz Nixdorf Forum (o.D.). *Die Welt im Netz – Die Geschichte des Internets.* https://www.hnf.de/dauerausstellung/ausstellungsbereiche/global-digital/die-welt-im-netz-die-geschichte-des-internets.html. Download 16.3.2025.
Statista (2025). *Worldwide internet user penetration from 2014 to February 2025.* https://www.statista.com/statistics/325706/global-internet-user-penetration/. Download 4.3.2025.
Statista (2024). *Share of households with internet access in Germany from 2010 to 2023.* https://www.statista.com/statistics/377677/household-internet-access-in-germany/#:~:text=In%202022%2C%20the%20share%20of,unchanged%20at%20around%2091.41%20percen. Download 4.3.2025.
United Nations. (o.D.). *Child and Youth Safety Online.* https://www.un.org/en/global-issues/child-and-youth-safety-online. Download 16.3.2025.

26 Reisen ins Ausland / Travel abroad
UN Tourism (former World Tourism Organization) (2025). *International tourism recovers pre-pandemic levels in 2024.* https://www.unwto.org/news/international-tourism-recovers-pre-pandemic-levels-in-2024. Download 18.3.2025.
UN Tourism (former World Tourism Organization) (2025). *Sustainable Development Goals (SDGs).* https://www.unwto.org/tourism-statistics/economic-contribution-SDG. Download 16.3.2025.

27 Smartphones / Smartphones
Boston University College of Communication (2018). *The Past, Present, and Future of Smartphone.* https://sites.bu.edu/cmcs/2018/09/14/the-past-present-and-future-of-smartphone/. Download 16.3.2025.
Statista (2024). *Telecommunication: Number of smartphone users worldwide from 2014 to 2029 (in millions).* https://www.statista.com/forecasts/1143723/smartphone-users-in-the-world. Download 4.3.2025.

Statista (2024). *Anteil der Smartphone-Nutzer* in Deutschland in den Jahren 2012 bis 2023 und Prognose bis 2030*. https://de.statista.com/statistik/daten/studie/585883/umfrage/anteil-der-smartphone-nutzer-in-deutschland/. Download 4.3.2025.

University of California (2017). *Your smartphone's hidden history*. https://www.universityofcalifornia.edu/news/your-smartphones-hidden-history. Download 16.3.2025.

28 Autos / Cars

Polst, Svenja, Patrick Mennig, Anna Schmitt und Katrin Scholz (2022). *„Mobilitätswende 2030". Vom Linienbus zur öffentlichen Mobilität der Zukunft*. Fraunhofer IESE, Kaiserslautern. https://www.iese.fraunhofer.de/content/dam/iese/publikation/smart-region-mobilitaetswende-2030-fraunhofer-iese.pdf. Download 16.3.2025.

Statista (2024). *Weltweiter Kfz-Bestand bis 2020*. https://de.statista.com/statistik/daten/studie/244999/umfrage/weltweiter-pkw-und-nutzfahrzeugbestand/#:~:text=Mehr%20Fahrzeuge%20weltweit%20als%20je,global%20registrierten%20Kraftfahrzeuge%20kontinuierlich%20an. Download 16.3.2025.

Statista (2021). *Bevölkerung in Deutschland nach Anzahl der PKW im Haushalt von 2018 bis 2021 (Personen in Millionen)*. https://de.statista.com/statistik/daten/studie/172093/umfrage/anzahl-der-pkw-im-haushalt/. Download 4.3.2025.

Statista (2015). *Percentage of households owning a car in selected countries in 2014, by country*. https://www.statista.com/statistics/516280/share-of-households-that-own-a-passenger-vehicle-by-country/. Download 4.3.2025.

29 CO_2-Emissionen / CO_2 emisssions

Chancel, Lucas, Thomas Piketty, Emmanuel Saez und Gabriel Zucman (2021). *World Inequality Report 2022*. Paris. https://wir2022.wid.world/www-site/uploads/2021/12/WorldInequalityReport2022_Full_Report.pdf. Download 4.3.2025.

European Youth Portal (2024). *How to reduce my carbon footprint?* https://youth.europa.eu/get-involved/sustainable-development/how-reduce-my-carbon-footprint_en. Download 16.3.2025.

University of California (2017). *Where do greenhouse gas emissions come from?* https://www.universityofcalifornia.edu/news/where-do-greenhouse-gas-emissions-come. Download 16.3.2025.

30 Bedrohung durch den Klimawandel / Threats from climate change

European Commission (2023). *DG Research and Innovation welcomes the Intergovernmental Panel on Climate Change (IPCC) report*. https://research-and-innovation.ec.europa.eu/news/all-research-and-innovation-news/dg-research-and-innovation-welcomes-intergovernmental-panel-climate-change-ipcc-report-2023-03-20_en#:~:text=Sea%20level%20rise%20is%20unavoidable,highly%20vulnerable%20to%20climate%20change. Download 4.3.2025.

World Bank Group (2022). *What you need to know about food security and climate change*. https://www.worldbank.org/en/news/feature/2022/10/17/what-you-need-to-know-about-food-security-and-climate-change. Download 16.3.2025.

31 Leben in Konfliktregionen / Life in conflict regions

Caravaggio Isabella, und Gregory Connor (2023). *Five things to know about the New Agenda for Peace. United Nations Development Programme*. https://www.undp.org/blog/five-things-know-about-new-agenda-peace#:~:text=Twenty%2Dfive%20percent%20of%20the,since%20the%20second%20world%20war. Download 4.3.2025.

Heidelberg Institute for International Conflict Research (HIIK) (2024). *Conflict Barometer 2023*. Heidelberg. https://hiik.de/konfliktbarometer/aktuelle-ausgabe/. Download 16.3.2025.

32 Demokratien und Autokratien / Democracies and autocracies

Gabler Wirtschaftslexikon (2018). *Demokratie*. https://wirtschaftslexikon.gabler.de/definition/demokratie-30416/version-253998. Download 16.3.2025.

Gabler Wirtschaftslexikon (2018). *Gewaltenteilung*. https://wirtschaftslexikon.gabler.de/definition/gewaltenteilung-33241/version-256768. Download 16.3.2025.

Gabler Wirtschaftslexikon (2018). *Indirekte Demokratie*. https://wirtschaftslexikon.gabler.de/definition/indirekte-demokratie-33370/version-256897. Download 16.3.2025.

Our World in Data (2025). *People living in democracies and autocracies, World*. https://ourworldindata.org/grapher/people-living-in-democracies-autocracies. Download 4.3.2025.

V-Dem Institute (2023). *Democracy Report 2023. Defiance in the Face of Autocratization*. Göteborg. https://www.v-dem.net/documents/29/V-dem_democracyreport2023_lowres.pdf. Download 4.3.2025.

33 Sicherheit / Safety

United Nations (2022). *The Sustainable Development Goals Report 2022*. New York. S. 58–59: Goal 16. https://unstats.un.org/sdgs/report/2022/The-Sustainable-Development-Goals-Report-2022.pdf. Download 18.3.2025.

34 Bürgerliche Freiheiten / Civil liberties

Freedom House (2025). *Countries and Territories*. https://freedomhouse.org/countries/freedom-world/scores. Download 4.3.2025.

35 Zugang zum Rechtsstaat / Access to rule of law

Independent Evaluation Office (IEO) of the United Nations Development Programme (UNDP) (2023). *Evaluation of the UNDP Support to Access to Justice*. o.O. https://erc.undp.org/evaluation/documents/download/22269. Download 4.3.2025.

36 Akademische Freiheit / Academic freedom

Friedrich-Alexander-Universität Erlangen-Nürnberg (2023). *Academic freedom deteriorates in 22 countries. Researchers at the University of Gothenburg and FAU Erlangen-Nürnberg publish the Academic Freedom Index 2023 Update*. https://www.fau.eu/2023/03/news/research/academic-freedom-deteriorates-in-22-countries/. Download 4.3.2025.

Gabler Wirtschaftslexikon (2022). *Wissenschaftsfreiheit*. https://wirtschaftslexikon.gabler.de/definition/wissenschaftsfreiheit-121063/version-385416. Download 16.3.2025.

37 Pressefreiheit / Freedom of the press

Reporters without borders (2025). *Global score (2023)*. https://rsf.org/en/index?year=2023. Download 4.3.2025.

Reporter ohne Grenzen (o.D.). *Informationsfreiheit im Internet*. https://www.reporter-ohne-grenzen.de/themen/internetfreiheit. Download 18.3.2025.

Reporter ohne Grenzen (o.D.). *Pressefreiheit – warum?* https://www.reporter-ohne-grenzen.de/themen/pressefreiheit-warum. Download 16.3.2025.

38 Korruption / Corruption

Transparency International (2025). *Corruption Perceptions Index (2023)*. https://www.transparency.org/en/cpi/2023?gclid=EAIaIQobChMI5M7_kLWWhAM-V0kJBAh1aPwH9EAAYAiAAEgI0NfD_BwE&gad_source=1. Download 4.3.2025.

Transparency International (2019). *25 corruption scandals that shook the world*. https://www.transparency.org/en/news/25-corruption-scandals. Download 18.3.2025.

39 Geschlechtergerechtigkeit / Gender equality

World Bank Group (2023). *Women, Business and the Law 2023*. Washington D.C. https://openknowledge.worldbank.org/server/api/core/bitstreams/b60c615b-09e7-46e4-84c1-bd5f4ab88903/content. Download 4.3.2025.

40 Gleichgeschlechtliche Ehe / Same-sex marriage

ILGA World database (2024). *Legal Frameworks. Criminalisation of consensual same-sex sexual acts*. https://database.ilga.org/criminalisation-consensual-same-sex-sexual-acts. Download 4.3.2025.

Pew Research Center (2024). *Same-Sex Marriage Around the World*. https://www.pewresearch.org/religion/fact-sheet/gay-marriage-around-the-world/. Download 4.3.2025.

Angaben zur Weltbevölkerung in unterschiedlichen Jahren durch World Bank Group:
World Bank Group (2025). *Population, total*. https://data.worldbank.org/indicator/SP.POP.TOTL. Download 4.3.2025.